MODERN DIESEL
LOCOMOTIVES

HANS HALBERSTADT

Motorbooks International
Publishers & Wholesalers

Dedication

For my dear friends and co-conspirators, Robin and Robert Genat.

First published in 1996 by Motorbooks International Publishers & Wholesalers, 729 Prospect Avenue, PO Box 1, Osceola, WI 54020-0001 USA

© Hans Halberstadt, 1996

Motorbooks International books are also available at discounts in bulk quantity for industrial or sales-promotional use. For details write to Special Sales Manager at the Publisher's address

Library of Congress Cataloging-in-Publication Data

Halberstadt, Hans
    Modern diesel locomotives / Hans Halberstadt.
        p. cm.   --(Motorbooks International
    enthusiast color series)
        Includes index.
        ISBN 0-7603-0199-9 (pbk. : alk. paper)
        1. Diesel locomotives--United States. I. Title.
        II. Series: Enthusiast color series.
    TJ619.H25 1996
    625.2'66--dc20   96-13070

On the front cover: The EMD SD70MAC, one of the most sophisticated of today's diesel locomotives.

On the frontispiece: A signal light.

On the title page: Burlington Northern's 9400 is a SD70MAC. The sunrise catches 9400 at Monument, Colorado, northbound from Pueblo to Denver.

On the back cover: Santa Fe's 862 streaming through Kingman Canyon in Arizona. *Howard Ande*

Printed in Hong Kong

Contents

Acknowledgments

The business of building a book is often a team sport where the author only really functions as the quarterback or coach. That has certainly been the case with this unusual railroad book. It could not have been built without the active assistance of many people—most within the railroad industry—who shared insights, experiences, and technical data with me. Others, particularly at Santa Fe, Amtrak, CalTrain, and Southern Pacific, provided that ultimate privilege, the "cab ride" in a rich variety of locomotives. I am extremely grateful, both to the organizations and to the individuals who assisted me in this project:

Southern Pacific Lines—Jack Martin, Scott Lewis, Don Seil, Richard Adams, Jim Johnson/Operation Lifesaver, and all the folks at the Roseville Locomotive Plant.

Atchison, Topeka & Santa Fe Railroad—Mike Martin; Monte Johnson; Jack Kahler; Ted Turner; Special Agent Brian Madden; engineers Stephen Priest, Jason Crupper, and Mel Wilson; plus the friendly folks at the Topeka shops and the Kansas City Argentine LMIT maintenance facility.

Amtrak—engineer Jeff Garrett and Supervisor Michael McBride; thanks for the ride and the insights.

CalTrain—Ed Gibson and Pat West, two guys who run trains on one of the oldest, heaviest-traveled commuter rail corridors in the United States.

Dave Crammer, rail industry journalist; thanks for the generous guidance and contacts.

Mike Green, who shared his extensive knowledge and research library.

Bruce Shelton, rail industry advocate and visionary; thanks for keeping this book on track.

And to the best rail magazine available, *Pacific Rail News*, particularly to editor Brian Solomon and contributors Howard Ande and Sean Graham-White, for their marvelous photography and superb cooperation.

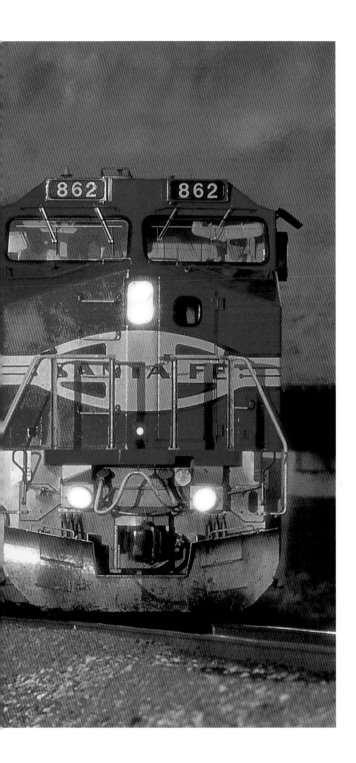

CHAPTER ONE

Power on the Point

The two-hour call comes at all hours of the day and night, from the operating department "crew callers" of dozens of railroads, on hundreds of subdivisions, to thousands of train engineers and conductors across Canada and the United States. They work for Conrail, Burlington Northern and Santa Fe, Canadian Pacific, Amtrak, Norfolk Southern, CSX, Southern Pacific, the little New England Central, and the vast Union Pacific. Thousands of times a day, all across North America, the crews report, sign in, collect the Haz Paks, general orders, superintendent's notices, track bulletins, and warrants. They haul their grips up to the cabs of a rich variety of motive power—ancient and grimy GP7s from the 1950s, speedy FL9 passenger locomotives, SD40-2s by the thousands, and the huge, muscular new freight engines such as the AC4400CWs and SD70MACs— and prepare for a day's work.

Here comes Santa Fe's 862 West on a scorching September evening at Kingman Canyon, Arizona. *Howard Ande*

The engineers settle in over on the right side of their cabs, insert the reverser in its receptacle, look over the instruments, check to see if the locomotives have had the required 24 hour federal inspection, and pour a cup of coffee from their Thermos. Each tests the train-line air brakes, listens to the radio for the call, "Got a good set and release," and then, "Highball from the car department! Have a good trip."

Each watches the block signal down the track turn from red to a permissive indication,

Santa Fe 819 is the power on the point for the hotshot train called the "QNYLA," pausing for 15 minutes at Kansas City's Argentine Yard fuel racks for a fill-up, a fresh crew, and servicing. The QNYLA is a "quality" train, a high-priority freight running across America, from New York to Los Angeles. As a hotshot, QNYLA gets nothing but the best in go-power—819 is a GE Dash 8-40CW, built in 1992.

Three westbounds pause at Kansas City's Union Pacific yards along the Kansas River—a portrait of real-world diesel locomotive technology today. Waiting for a fresh crew before continuing its westward journey, UP 9423 is a GE Dash 8, a very popular design. On the right is a EMD SD60M trailing a mile or so of empty coal cars, returning to Wyoming for another load.

Santa Fe 5815 is a muscular SD45-2, hustling eastbound across Kansas, approaching Emporia at sunrise on an August morning with a mixed freight. The SD45-2 looks pretty much like any other diesel-electric of its vintage, but under that long hood lurks one of the biggest engine blocks around, a V-20 displacing almost 13,000 cubic inches.

It's 0600 hours in Winnemucca, Nevada, and Amtrak has just arrived—only 20 minutes late. Head-end power is a pair of F40PH locomotives, a light, fast, and (for a locomotive) agile design from the 1970s and 1980s.

then moves the reverser to Forward and the throttle to Run 1. Each monitors the ammeter as the needle climbs toward 1000 amps, typically controlling the load at around 600 amps. And each modulates the independent brakes to keep slack from running out too fast, thus pulling the train in two. At all hours, in all kinds of weather, the people who run the trains listen to the massive diesel engines rev up and the turbochargers whine and feel the steel wheels turn. The trains slowly start to move, taking with them all kinds of goods to all kinds of places all across the North American continent. The throttles ease forward, one notch at a time: Run 2, Run 3, up to Run 8, full blast. Another trip begins for the people who run the trains.

Diesel Locomotion Today

These locomotives provide the "power on the point" for the "hot-shot" fast freights, for the heavy coal and iron-ore trains, for the little "dog" locals, and for the commuter trains in New York, Los Angeles, and San Francisco. They work the "hump" and move the cuts of cars in the big Argentine Yard at Kansas City and at dozens of other small places where trains are built and switched out.

They move almost everything that keeps the North American economy alive and well: automobiles; chemicals; coal; wheat by the trainload; raw logs and finished lumber; gold, silver, iron, tungsten, and aluminum ore headed for the smelter; refined metals headed for factories; and finished goods headed for market. Trains also haul container loads of Asian-manufactured computers, televisions, and clothing across the "land bridge" from West Coast ports to the eastern ports of New York, and on to Europe.

These locomotives, even the smallest, are huge in every respect. They weigh around a quarter of a million pounds, often much more. Some of them consume fuel from 5,000-gallon tanks at a rate of three or four gallons per mile. New ones cost $2 million plus. When they finally die and go

Here comes a revolution up the hill—a set of Burlington Northern's huge fleet of new SD70MACs, the first really new locomotives in many years. Three MACs pull a loaded coal train up from Monument, Colorado, to the pass at Palmer Lake, Colorado, a grade that previously required five SD40-2s. The MACs use AC traction motors, a new electrical system, and self-steering axles to provide dramatically improved tractive power.

above
Amtrak 814 is a Genesis locomotive—the design voted "Most Ugly" in a recent survey. Beneath the stainless steel cowl body lurks the heart and soul of a GE Dash 8, a fine locomotive with an excellent reputation for performance and reliability. Here, the 814 stops at the fuel pits for a fill-up; then it is off again.

right
You won't see these locomotives pulling freights very often. They're F40PH models from EMD—very fast, light power designed for the many starts and stops of commuter rail service.

off to the scrapper's torch, each has typically traveled millions of miles. But for all their huge bulk and cost, they shrink the price of what we pay for everything we use—clothes, heat, light, food, computers, and even books about locomotives.

These locomotives—even the oldest of them—are really relatively new machines. The first one appeared on the market in 1925, and the first main-line designs only became widely available about 50 years ago. That original concept was so valid that even a half century of development has—until recently—only produced incremental improvements rather than radical change. It was a tool so nearly perfect in design that nearly new, state-of-the-art steam locomotives were scrapped in favor of smaller, weaker diesel-electrics just as soon as the manufacturers could crank them out of the factories.

But finally, a radical design change has occurred. In 1993, the first really new kind of locomotive, the General Motors (GM) Electro-Motive Division (EMD) SD70MAC, hit the rails. Now the whole railroad industry (particularly the locomotive-building part) is suddenly in a period of transformation. These new alternating-current (AC) locomotives offer radically improved performance: Five of the new locomotives can replace *nine* of the old ones! That is nearly a one-for-two ratio, and that's

Joyce is an apprentice "hostler," learning to run locomotives by helping to move them around the yard for servicing; she is entering the pipeline that will train her to someday join the ranks of the engineers. She learns the trade by beginning with hooking up cuts of cars in the Roseville, California, yard, setting switches and brakes.

F59PHI number 2003 uses B-type trucks—two axles instead of three, as on the "C" type.

The 1530 hours Capitol, with a new F59PHI on the point, dashes past at speed. The EMD F59 is a modern passenger locomotive incorporating many of the computer-based technologies of the newer AC models but with conventional DC traction systems.

Despite the fresh, glittering paint, Santa Fe 2841 is an ancient locomotive with a million (or two) miles on the odometer. It is a GP35 originally built in the mid-1960s, rebuilt about 15 years later. Despite its antiquity, 2841 serves in the yard at Emporia, Kansas, where one crew quits for the day and another gets ready to take over for the evening's work.

the kind of thing that makes the folks who run railroads sit up and take notice. Burlington Northern signed up for 350 of them, right out of the box—at almost $2 million per copy. The Southern Pacific and Union Pacific are buying them, too.

This is an exciting time to watch trains. But diesel-electric locomotives have always been pretty interesting. They've been evolving from the little ugly ducklings of the early years, to the mature—and hated—technology that displaced steam, to the fascinating, huge, glittering modern machines such as the SD70MAC, which is currently transforming the industry. Here's how it happened.

18

Way up in the wild, remote northeastern corner of California is the little village called Nubieber. Once a major crew-change point, Nubieber now serves just one train a day. Today's visitor is an SD40-2, the most common locomotive in North America. Union Pacific owns almost 1,100 of the breed, but there are thousands more running the rails in the United States and Canada.

above
A rather new Dash 9 with a load of "double-stacks" in tow stops for a crew change at Union Pacific's Green River, Wyoming, facility. Another westbound, led by an old SD50, also waits for its new crew before pressing on over the Continental Divide.

left
Jeff Garrett at the helm of Amtrak 722, eastbound out of El Sobrante, California, and winding up toward 70 miles per hour. The F59PHI's cockpit uses desktop controls quite different in configuration (but not function) from those on older locomotives. The "Whisper Cab" is quieter than those of earlier models—but it is still pretty noisy at speed.

Santa Fe 690 is a Dash 9 in "war bonnet" livery, roaring up from San Bernardino, California, toward the fabled Cajon Pass. Cajon is the bottleneck most rail traffic must negotiate before entering the Los Angeles basin. The grade is steep, and runaways on the westbound run are fairly common. But now it takes all the 12,000 horsepower produced by three units in Run 8—full throttle—to get up and over the hill.

next pages
Can it be? Yes, it really is Burlington Northern's 9400, the official "class" or "first" SD70MAC, complete with chromed handrails and a little plaque proclaiming its status, grinding up toward Palmer Lake. Although not the first MAC to hit the rails, 9400 is the ceremonial granddaddy of the family, the one christened by Burlington Northern's chairman, Gerald Grinstein, on 10 January 1994. Now 9400 works for a living, just like the rest of the fleet—but it's the only one with chromed hand rails. The sunrise catches 9400 at Monument, Colorado, northbound from Pueblo to Denver, with a long string of empties.

Drifting down slope from Tehachapi to Mojave, California, one of Southern Pacific's extensive tribe of SD45T-2s brakes before entering the yard and then pressing on toward Cajon Pass to the south. The T is a variation of the SD45T-2 almost unique to the Southern Pacific, a version with radiator air inlets lower than normal. Southern Pacific locomotives spend a lot of time in tunnels; hot exhaust from the lead units gets trapped at the roof of the tunnel and overheats trailing locomotives inside long tunnels, so the intakes were repositioned so that they inhale air from the sides, rather than from on top.

24

above
Massachusetts Bay Transportation Authority
F-40s, complete with "ghetto bars" to protect the
crews from flying bricks, stand by at South
Station in downtown Boston. *Brian Solomon*

right
Back to the future, part F40. Engineer Pat West
runs the train from the cab car at the rear; the
F40PH locomotive is five cars back. Pat is
accelerating through 65 miles per hour toward 70
on this stretch of track along the San Francisco
Peninsula. This line has been in passenger service
since 1864—and the 50-mile trip still takes just
about the same time as it did during the Civil War
(1-1/2 hours now, 2 hours then).

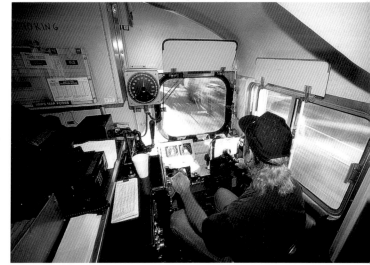

CHAPTER TWO

The Locomotive Industry

Until a few years ago the North American locomotive industry was in a dreary, sad state. One after another, legendary names well-known for steam designs faded out of the industry: Baldwin, the American Locomotive Company (ALCO), Lima Hamilton, Fairbanks-Morse (a diesel-only builder), all gone. Today there are only two *real* players left in the game, each a giant—General Motors' (GM) Electro-Motive Division (EMD), and General Electric (GE) Transportation Systems.

It looks like a Dash 9, sounds like a Dash 9, but it is the new AC4400CW from GE, grinding up the hill in Run 8 with thousands of tons of coal cars astern. The AC4400CW uses AC locomotive technology to produce 4,000 to 4,400 horsepower converted to 145,000 pounds of draw bar pull.

They called the SD9 the "Cadillac," mostly for its smooth, comfortable ride when they hit the rails back in the mid-1950s. The SD is for "special duty," and the SD9 improved on the SD7, which was the first of EMD's six-axle "hood" diesel-electric locomotives, a hard-working, durable concept. Today's SD70MAC is really a direct descendant of this excellent locomotive.

Until 1983, EMD totally dominated the market, typically selling about 60 percent of all locomotives every year. But that wasn't enough for GM—EMD was up for sale, a marginally profitable operation. Then things got interesting: GE's Dash 8, a solid, conventional direct-current (DC) locomotive with some unconventional improvements, started outselling EMD's line. General Electric's Dash 8 was a wake-up call for EMD, and EMD responded with a renewed commitment to compete and transform the industry. The competition resulted in steady improvements in locomotive performance, culminating in EMD's introduction of the first production AC locomotive to go into widespread use. In the years since, both companies have introduced radically new AC models with far more power than DC units. Although the new units are exquisitely expensive, the railroads are buying them in huge numbers because they can replace older models on an almost one-for-two basis. These new models—such as the SD70MAC and the AC4400CW—are quickly displacing huge fleets of power in some parts of the United States and Canada, changing the look of the railroads. And (for the moment) neither company can churn out these big locomotives fast enough to fill the steady stream of incoming orders.

Evolution of the Modern Locomotive

One of the many charms of watching trains is the rich variety of power on the "point." Just visit one of the hot spots or rework facilities and observe the progress of locomotive technology over the past few decades. It is quite common to see locomotives in action along the main line, in the yards, and particularly along branch lines, that are at least 20, and often 30 years old. In any other industry, these machines would have been recycled into washing machines or tin cans, but the railroads keep them going until the wheels are ready to fall off. Southern Pacific's Roseville Locomotive Shops has a nice collection of first-generation GP7s on the property. Santa Fe's Huge Argentine Yard in Kansas City, Kansas, and Barstow Yard in Barstow, California, are almost totally run by small fleets of second-generation SD39s that the railroad has thoroughly rebuilt.

Locomotive Basics

Electric locomotives appeared as an alternative to the tried and true steam locomotives around the end of the previous century. The city of New York banned steam locomotives from its bor-

Here's what the first main-line diesel-electric locomotives to see widespread service looked like, EMD's classic, still-beautiful F-series. This one is an FP7 on the point of Southern Pacific's Train No. 13, the "Shasta Daylight," and it is a fairly late example of the design that stayed in production for more than a quarter-century, from 1937 to 1963.

ders in the 1880s because of the smoke and fumes produced by these engines. Electric power was the only alternative, and at first that power came from overhead wires and "third" current-carrying rails.

Wires and current-carrying rails are very expensive to install and maintain. Direct diesel and gasoline power with mechanical drive trains were tested in dozens of configurations. The diesel electric was just one of these, the one that worked the best.

A diesel electric seems like a goofy way to produce tractive power, but it works better than anything else for huge vehicles. The process begins with a big diesel engine directly connected to a generator (for a DC loco) or an alternator (for an AC system). The generator or alternator converts the power of the engine from torque to current. The current flows through the engineer's controls to very large motors hung on each of the locomo-

Santa Fe 2769 is another bit of working history, a GP30 from the early 1950s. Now consigned to puttering around the huge Argentine Yard in Kansas City, the GP7s following represent the first generation of diesel-electric power after the age of steam.

tive's axles and the motors convert the current to torque again, driving the wheels through simple spur gears.

Why not a mechanical drive? The components become too big, the torque curve is jagged, and you'd need a clutch the size of Cleveland to get a typical freight train moving. Also, the tremendous torque required would try to tip a mechanical-drive locomotive on its side when starting (as a car's engine does in a small way, too), but the electric-drive forces tend to push the locomotive forward.

Radical Changes in Railroading

This is an exciting time for railroading. Not only is the industry resurgent, with traffic and profits way up and the Class 1 (major) railroads healthier than they've been in decades, but the technology of locomotion has changed drastically in the last few years. Computers are part of the change, but the big reason is a new kind of traction motor system based on AC instead of DC technology. Alternating current, along with computer control and other features, has essentially *doubled* the pulling ability of a 4,000-horsepower diesel engine in a locomotive. This improvement has resulted in huge orders of new locomotives by most of the major railroads, particularly the ones that pull coal trains up mountainsides. But AC's extra tractive effort comes at a cost; these locomotives are expensive—about $2.5 million a copy. For trains that run on the flat, conventional DC locomotives still make sense and still sell well. General Electric's Dash 8 and Dash 9 are extremely modern locomotives and both use traditional DC traction systems, at about $1.8 million in 1996.

Burlington Northern accepted four AC-powered SD60MACs for testing and put them to work hauling coal on the challenging run from Wyoming's Powder River Basin down to electrical power stations in Texas. These were the first freight AC locomotive demonstraters. Burlington Northern found it could use just three SD60MAC locomotives instead of the five DC-powered EMD SD40-2s they needed before—and they could get over the pass at Palmer Lake, Colorado, without the pushers needed with earlier power. Not only that, when the pencil-pushers got done scribbling, the MACs had a 10–15 percent fuel economy advantage over the conventional DC version of the SD60MAC, the SD60, and Burlington Northern was convinced.

The EMD SD70MAC's engine is the 16-710G3B-EC with 710 cubic inches per cylinder; 16 cylinders with a total displacement of 11,360 cubic inches (although locomotive displacement is normally specified in individual cylinders, rather than total). That's fed by an electronic fuel injection system and the whole thing is good for about 4,000 horsepower. Now, 4,000 horsepower is not much more than the 3,600 horsepower EMD and GE engines have been pumping out for decades—difference is that these horses pull on the draw bar with 137,000 pounds of force, far more than the SD40s, 45s, Dash 7s, and Dash 8s that gulp about the same amount of fuel.

EMD Locomotives

The giant manufacturing company that has dominated the locomotive industry for so many years started out in 1922 as the Electro-Motive Corporation (EMC until 1930, EMD ever since), an obscure little business on the sixth floor of a Detroit office building. EMD designed and built little gasoline- and diesel-electric rail cars—a kind of bus or interurban vehicle designed to run on the rails. It was a classic little niche market, and EMC's products fit perfectly. Even during the depth of the Depression, EMC's and EMD's rail cars sold well—over 500 between 1922 and 1930.

EMC bought its engines from the Winton Engine Company, the designer and manufacturer of a lightweight diesel engine. Neither company rated much more than a footnote in the locomotive industry press of the early

The Union Pacific is the one railroad in America with a sense of history and a program to preserve its role in the past. Here is part of that program, and railroad history—an E-series locomotive restored by Union Pacific, nose-to-nose with a Dash 8. This E9 is part of an A-B-A set (two locomotives with control cabs, plus an auxiliary unit in between) frequently used to pull executive cars for inspection tours around the huge Union Pacific system, and part of a larger preservation program that includes other important locomotives.

31

1920s. That era was heavily dominated by big steam engines from Baldwin, ALCO, and the other historic locomotive builders.

But the GM company decided to get into the locomotive manufacturing business in 1930—and they weren't going to get steamed up about it, either. Since the successful introduction of the diesel-electric by ALCO, GE, and Ingersoll-Rand six years previous, the concept of diesel had proven efficient, economical, and promising. General Motors had the financial muscle from its many enterprises to buy into the diesel-electric industry—which it exercised by purchasing EMC and Winton in 1930, forming EMD.

The new enterprise began work on ambitious new design concepts; locomotives much bigger, faster, and imaginative than the little diesel-electric switchers then in use. It took four years, but the result was a product that essentially blew the doors off the competition—the Chicago, Burlington & Quincy Railroad *Pioneer Zephyr*.

The *Zephyr* was true to its name, a sleek, stainless steel, three-car train set built ostensibly for Burlington but really aimed at the imagination of the American public. It was a direct hit! It was, by today's standards, a little train: only 600 horsepower, with just two traction motors (in the leading trucks), and accommodating a mere 72 passengers. But it was good for 110 miles per hour, had remarkable endurance, and—most important—looked terrific. Everybody wanted a ride. Well, the steam locomotive manufacturers didn't know it, but they were on their way out of business. Smelly, sooty steamers looked clunky in comparison. The *Zephyr* was cheap to buy, to operate, and to maintain. Suddenly, the big steam locomotives started to look dreary and old-fashioned.

The *Zephyr* served as a technology demonstrator for years, setting the stage for high-speed passenger trains with diesel power. It was the first diesel passenger train in the United States in regular scheduled service, with a daily run between Kansas City, Missouri, and Lincoln, Nebraska. Operating expenses turned out to be half of those of a steam locomotive on the same run, $0.34 per mile for the *Zephyr*, $0.64 per mile for steam power.

Other *Zephyrs* entered passenger service and were a huge success; the demand for seats exceeded capacity, the new trains knocked hours off the old steam schedules, and made money for their lines right out of the box. The original *Pioneer Zephyr* is now a static display in a museum.

The E Series and F Series Locomotives

General Motors' commitment to EMD included a large investment in both research and development. They put big bucks into facilities, and spent the time needed to plan the

It looks like a new locomotive—and it pulls like one, too—but 6936 is the last of its tribe still in service. This locomotive is a huge Centennial, with two big diesel engines supplying 6,600 horsepower, eight powered axles, and what looks like a modern wide cab. Although preserved by Union Pacific as part of its collection of historic power, 6936 can still be found working freight trains around the system, just as in its glory days.

This GP30 was hot stuff back in the early 1960s when it was new. Santa Fe rebuilt them all after about 20 years, but 2742's days are numbered. It will be replaced by an SD39 or B-23-7 one of these days; then it will be sent off to be cut up for scrap.

best way to make and market a new kind of head-end power. The division got a new factory in 1936, built at La Grange, Illinois, near Chicago. A year later, in 1937, a completely new kind of locomotive, the sleek, substantial E series, rolled out onto the test track and off into the real world.

This revolutionary locomotive used two EMD 900-horsepower engines, each a big V-12 based on the two-stroke-cycle design, pressure charged (a kind of low-pressure turbo-charging), each cylinder displacing 567 cubic inches for a total displacement of 6,804 cubic inches. That engine powered two types of units: an A type

General Electric's workhorse locomotive has been, for many years, the C30-7 (sometimes called the Dash 7, but only by GE). The crew of Burlington Northern 5040 are using the RamAire® ventilation system on this scorching August morning, but it isn't helping much because they're only moving at a walk. The 1980-vintage C30-7s replaced the SD9s of the 1950s—and are now being retired in turn.

with a control cab and a B type without controls. Normally two As could travel with B units sandwiched in-between. The whole lash-up was in essence a 5,400-plus-horsepower rocket that soon powered the premium passenger trains of the day. The E series was designed primarily for passenger service, with a steam power system to provide light and heat in the passenger cars.

The E series stayed in production for over a quarter century, with the E9—the final version E series locomotive—being produced

through 1963. Some are still running, including one A-B-A set (an A unit has a control cab plus the powerplant and drive train, a B unit is just a power unit used to provide more go-power; an A-B-A lash-up has one B unit sandwiched between two As) restored and used regularly by the Union Pacific. These are very important locomotives: They set the basic standard for mainline diesel-electric power—for economy, reliability, practicality, and power. During their 27 years of production, Es and Fs received an upgraded engine and numerous smaller improvements. This development program rapidly transformed GM's EMD from a brash newcomer to the dominant force in American locomotive technology—and EMD sold more than 7,300 units. It was one of those major milestones in engineering achievement that shaped history.

Dick Dilworth's Ugly Duckling: The GP Locomotives

As lovely as the Es and Fs were (and are) they are a bit under-powered. Also, the full-cowl construction, which supported the prime mover and parts like a truss bridge and thus had no underframe, made access to the engine, generator, compressor, electrical systems, and related components rather more difficult than necessary. And the fully cowled body did look great with a passenger train. After the war, while the conversion from steam to diesel was going strong, EMD started another development program for a new kind of locomotive, a stronger, simpler, multi-purpose machine that could do anything for anybody and cost less, to boot.

The senior designer on the team was Dick Dilworth, a man with a dream. It was really more like a nightmare, according to Dilworth, who said, "I wanted to make a locomotive so ugly in appearance that no railroad would want it on their main line or anywhere near their headquarters. But they would want it out as far as possible in the back country, where it could really do useful work. My second dream was to make it so simple in construction and so devoid of Christmas-tree ornaments and other whimsy that the price would be materially below our standard main-line freight locomotives."[1]

Dilworth was partly successful. The "Geep" (as everybody calls it, a nickname based on GP or General Purpose) was a stunningly ugly locomotive, the antithesis of the stylish F-series units. It was a locomotive so homely that no paint scheme could make it look good. It was almost as graceless as today's custom Amtrak locomotive, the AMD-

103 *Genesis.* But the ugly duckling was so darn *practical* that every railroad wanted a fleet of them.

The GP7 used a single 1,500-horsepower engine as its foundation, a substantial jolt of power at the time, applied to four traction motors, one on each axle. Instead of the full-cowl body used on the F-series, Dilworth's team gave the GP7 a "hood" type of body, with a narrow cover for the engine and full-width cab. The layout provided the crew with good visibility fore and aft, which meant that the GP7 could serve as a yard switcher, a road engine, or a passenger locomotive. While it lacked the sleek and aerodynamic lines of earlier designs, the access doors along the hood let mechanics access the locomotive's vitals to change out power assemblies or air components without major surgery.

Ugly or not, the first generation GP is perhaps the most successful locomotive of the diesel-electric age. With about 9,000 copies in several muta-

Union Pacific 5038 hustles eastward, accelerating out of the world's biggest yard complex at North Platte, Nebraska. This SD50 is a 3,600-horsepower DC locomotive weighing in at almost 400,000 pounds; Missouri Pacific bought 60 of them during the mid-1980s, and Union Pacific acquired them through a merger.

You wouldn't know it from this angle, but these two locomotives are pretty similar on the back side of the cab. The one on the left is a Dash 8 from GE, with the wide cab introduced by the Canadian manufacturer Montreal Locomotive Works. On the right is EMD's beloved GP60, a locomotive with a conventional cab. The wide cab adds a lot of weight to the front of the locomotive—and when it was tried with the GP60M, the result was a terrible ride. Santa Fe engineers often select the GP60 as an all-time favorite.

tions (through the GP18), the GP set the standard for diesel-electric freight locomotives that continues today. In fact, production of the GP continues today because Dilworth's ugly duckling is still rolling off the production line under other aliases. Under the sheet metal, today's SD70s and Dash 9s are essentially GP7s on steroids; the engines are bigger, some of the traction motors use AC instead of DC, there are computers in the cab, and the noses are sometimes wider (and warmer in winter), but the fundamentals are identical. And if you can run a GP7, as one Santa Fe

engineer said, you can run a Dash 9 or AC4400CWs. And a flock of the early models still nests alongside the engine house at Roseville, just in case they're needed. The GP series has evolved through many permutations and models: the GP7, 9, 18, 20, 28, 30, 35, 38, 39, 40, 40x, 49, 50, 59, and 60. The GP40x, GP50, and GP60 are perhaps the champions of the breed, favorites of many Santa Fe Railroad engineers across the Midwest and West. Said Stephen Priest, Atchison, Topeka & Santa Fe Railroad engineer who gets to run just about everything in the fleet:

Here comes an SD45T-2 around the bend at Walong, California, just downhill from the famed Tehachapi Loop. The SD45T-2 was hot stuff back in the early 1970s, and it remains a solid performer 25 years later, toward the end of its working life.

"My absolute *favorite* engine for running on the main line is the GP60, followed closely by the Dash 8-40B. These are both the last modern engines delivered *before* the new cab became standard, and they are wonderful—lots of horsepower, smooth transition, very comfortable for the crew. For a long time cabs were too cold in winter and too hot in summer—both problems resolved by the manufacturers with these and subsequent models.

"On the Santa Fe, the 100-series are the most-hated locomotives—the GP60Ms. This is odd because so many of us adore the GP60. The M is the wide-nose version of the model, and that's where the problem is. The cab is way too heavy for the suspension and so the locomotives beat you to death. You are constantly bounced around the cab, you feel every joint and jolt. But the standard Geep 60s ride perfectly! The extra mass of the cab, along with its weight distribution, are responsible for the terrible ride."

The SD Series DC-Powered Locomotives

The EMD Special Duty (SD) family of fine locomotives is based on the same technology and components used in the GPs—the same engines, alternators, and traction motors. The basic differ-

Union Pacific 9262 is one of that confusing Dash 8 clan from GE with the older, conventional cab. The Dash 8 can show up with a Canadian (also called "Safety," "Comfort," "Crew," or "Wide"—take your pick) cab or GE's version of the wide cab. A Dash 8 can be identified with a roster list or by counting the access doors and checking the positions of the inlets behind the cab.

ence is that all SDs have three-axle trucks as opposed to the two-axle trucks on all GPs. That means that the horsepower produced by the engine is split six ways rather than four. It also means the SDs are heavier—and heavier typically means better traction. If all these designations seem confusing, you aren't alone; all the SD series have six powered axles, all the GP series have four.

The SDs have been extremely popular, outselling the GPs by a wide margin. Both have their applications, but for most railroads, the six-motor SD design is the preferred locomotive. The series started with the SD7—a 1,500-horsepower, six-motor machine—in 1952 and has generally paralleled the GP series with equivalent models.

The most popular (in numbers sold) is the SD40 and SD40-2, a 3,000-horsepower locomotive based on the 16-cylinder version of the EMD 645E engine (645 cubic inches per cylinder).

Railroads in the United States and Canada bought over 4,500 of these locomotives during the 22 years EMD produced them, from 1966 to 1988.

But GM offered many SD designs, each with some incremental improvement, usually with more horsepower—and the crews that use them will sometimes come up with surprising preferences and dislikes. As Mel Wilson said, "My favorite locomotive is the SD-35. I used them when I worked on the Soo Line, hauling average kinds of freight trains—75 cars or so. That was all the power we had available for that train—and it was just wonderful! The engine is rated at 2,500 horsepower and it just seemed to fit what we were doing. You won't make any land speed records but the power was there when you needed it, and the locomotives were very sure-footed."

The Start of a New Era: The AC-Powered SD70MAC

The EMD SD70MAC has changed the railroad industry the same way the Boeing 707 changed commercial aviation: It was a dramatically improved product that provided much greater economy and efficiency.

Development began in 1989, with four SD60MACs, 3,800-horsepower demonstration units ready for testing in 1992. These four locomotives used a Siemens Transportation Systems rectifier and traction inverter, along with the EMD's new radial truck design. The test results with the demonstrators were amazing: starting tractive effort of 175,000 pounds and a continuous rating of 117,000 pounds.

The SD70MAC 16-cylinder engine displaces 710 cubic inches per cylinder and is fed by electronic fuel injection. The engine's 4,000 horsepower is only 400 more than the SD60, but the tractive effort is greatly increased, not to mention the fact that fuel consumption is about equal.

The SD70MAC's impressive figures were enough to convince Burlington Northern to place the largest locomotive order in history for 350 of EMD's SD70MAC.

Within the first few months of the SD70MAC's operation, Burlington Northern increased the order to 434. Burlington Northern found it could haul coal trains out of Wyoming's Powder River Basin with just three SD70MAC locomotives instead of the five SD40-2s they needed before, and they could get over the pass at Palmer Lake without the pushers needed with earlier power.

SD70MAC Specs & Performance

Diesel Engine Power: 4,000 horsepower
Tractive Effort (continuous): 137,000 pounds
Tractive Effort (starting): 175,000 pounds
Adhesion: 33 percent
Dynamic Brake: 81,000 pounds
Fuel Capacity: 5,000 gallons
Engine: 16 cylinders, 11,360 cubic inches, electronic fuel injection
Wheels: 42 inches
Trucks: Radial, self-steering
Sales (to June 1, 1995): 434

GE Diesel Division Locomotives

General Electric's Diesel Division has a long and illustrious role in the history of locomotion, long pre-dating the first production diesel-electric locomotive in 1924, but until 1953 GE was essentially a bit player in a performance starring EMD. That's surprising since GE had been designing and building state-of-the art electrical-power technology since the 19th century and was part of the joint venture that produced the first commercial diesel-electric, the ALCO No. 1.

General Electric's history in the electric-locomotion business goes back to 1880, shortly after the invention of the dynamo (in Italy in 1860 by Antonio Pacinotti), when Thomas A. Edison built and operated an experimental electric locomotive at his research facility at Menlo Park, New Jersey. In 1887, the Edison General Electric Company built a little 40-horsepower electric locomotive for use in mines.

Here's another Union Pacific Dash 8, this one with the wide-cab option.

General Electric was formally founded in 1892, a merger of Edison's company and the Thomason-Houston Company, another pioneer in electric motor development, and began selling switching locomotives of 1,440 horsepower plus a complete line of electric locomotives for mine use. In 1894 GE electrified the Grand Central Terminal in New York City and supplied 30 1,700-horsepower electric locomotives for the new system, and these sturdy, early locomotives stayed in service more than 70 years.

During the early decades of the 20th century, GE refined the use of electric traction systems for the railroad industry, but with a heavy emphasis on pure electrified systems. While pure electric power has many virtues, and still is predominant in parts of the eastern United States and across Europe and elsewhere, the cost of initial installation (with 600-volt overhead wires or third-rails) is about four times more expensive than conventional main-line development. The technology was highly competitive as long as steam technology was the only alternative; electric locomotives are tremendously pow-

Here is yet another version of the Dash 8, this one with B-type trucks. General Electric calls this the "Genesis" locomotive—most rail fans just call them ugly. But it zooms along in a respectable manner, and that's what counts. The Dash 8 Genesis is still in production, the latest main-line passenger locomotive.

erful, fast, reliable, and require little servicing. The assumption, by GE and many railroads, was that if anything was going to replace the steam engine it would be the straight electric locomotive—and they were right, too, for much of the industrialized world . . . except North America.

Although GE participated in the development of the ALCO No. 1, it was as a partner and supplier of the electrical components only, rather than as the primary manufacturer. While EMD was busy building prototypes and demonstrators of their diesel-electric design, then flooding the

right

Here comes an SD60M, easing down a grade in western Wyoming near the old railroad town of Evanston; the engineer has the dynamic brake set in "Dynamic" 8, and the locomotive whines downhill, digging in its heels to hold the heavy train. Although the wide Canadian cab became widely available in 1988, some models of passenger and freight locomotives included the bigger office much earlier.

The AC-powered SD70MAC is the most important development in diesel-electric technology in many decades—perhaps since the first DC model, the ALCO No. 1 of 1924.

market with the E and F series, GE continued working with ALCO, picking up the shreds of market share left from whatever EMD didn't sell. General Electric also experimented and innovated on its own, selling all kinds of fascinating systems, including the 4,500-horsepower gas-turbine/electric design ordered by Union Pacific in 1948 and the 11,000-horsepower straight electric locomotives for the Great Northern, but they didn't sell nearly as many units as EMD.

But by 1950 it was obvious to almost everybody that both steam power and pure electric power were technologies of the past for the broad open spaces of most of Canada and the United States. General Electric's response was to dive into the diesel-electric business, starting with its own design development program in 1952 and termination of its long relationship with ALCO in 1953. The company bought the rights to the proven Cooper-Bessemer FDL diesel engine and began building diesel-electric locomotives at Erie, Pennsylvania.

Soon, prototype main-line locomotives—two with 1,200-horsepower V-8 engines

Burlington Northern started the big switch to AC power with these SD70MACs, primarily for their many coal train runs from the Powder River basin of Wyoming to the power stations of the midwest.

and two with 1,800-horsepower V-12 engines—roamed the rails, beginning five years of testing on the Erie Railroad, from 1954 to 1959. The result was a new engine—a huge V-16, chock full of vitamins, pumping out 2,400 horsepower and totally outclassing EMD's 1,800- and 2,000-horsepower units.

The GE Universals: Attack of the U-Boats

General Electric's version of the main-line diesel-electric hit the rails in 1960, christened the U25B (Universal, 2,500-horsepower, B-type trucks), the first serious competitor to EMD's dominant GPs. The U25B sold well, 478 units during the first few years, and suddenly GE was the number-two vendor of diesel-electric locomotives in North America. Somebody called the design the "U-Boat," and it stuck. The design has been improved, expanded, and developed over the years—a solid success based on a solid foundation. Many in the Universal series are still earning their keep today, including a few of those first U25Bs.

continued on page 47

The SD80MAC, SD90MAC, and AC6000

New! Improved! More powerful than a speeding competitive locomotive! This is the new SD90MAC in Union Pacific's colors. Union Pacific is the only railroad to order EMD's 6,000-horsepower locomotives so far, and to get a jump on deliveries they're receiving them with the old 4,300-horsepower 710 engine. As soon as the new 6,000-horsepower "H" block is ready, EMD will swap the new block for the old one. *Sean Graham-White*

Just when we were all getting accustomed to the radical idea of 4,000 horsepower engines and trying to figure out how AC traction systems work their magic, just when railfans and railroad employees were getting used to the shock of the SD70MAC and then the AC4400, a whole new set of surprises came rumbling down the tracks from GE and EMD.

"The railroads thought the 4,000-horsepower locomotive was fine and dandy," said Sean Graham-White, Modern Power columnist for Pacific Rail News, "but they took a wait-and-see attitude about AC. They didn't see a huge difference in performance between a 4,000-horsepower DC and a 4,000-horsepower AC system. The railroads said, in effect, 'these 4,000-horsepower units are cute, but how about something that will give us a two-for-one ratio...how about 6,000 horsepower?' EMD and GE had been promoting AC technology, making a lot of claims, and the railroads said 'Prove it!'"

The SD70MAC proved the point, starting in 1994. The rated figures, including the official ones published in this book, are very conservative, according to industry observers. The actual performance, out in the real world, is far better than Burlington Northern expected or what the ratings promise.

There were developmental problems with a new technology—there always are, and they were anticipated—and there has been some negative press relating to troubles with the SD70MAC and AC4400. The first units were plagued with problems but, as EMD and BN climbed the learning curve, the MAC exceeded expectations. "The 'bean-counters' at BN are extremely happy," according to an industry source. Once they saw what AC units could do in the real world, many of the Class I railroads started placing orders for AC units with the biggest engines on anybody's drawing board.

"The new EMD SD90MAC and the GE AC6000 are really going to revolutionize American railroading," Sean says. "Conrail is already replacing *four* conventional locomotives on intermodal trains with *one* SD80MAC in tests!"

The implications of these very newest designs for railroad managers are interesting. For example, Union Pacific has 1,100 older 3,000-horsepower SD40-2 locomotives operating today. If the builder's claims of replacing units in a two to one ratio with a 6,000 horsepower locomotives are correct, it appears they could get away with something like half that number with the new units. These units are easier to maintain, are more reliable, and use less fuel. This is something that makes an accountant very happy. The problem, as of Spring 1996, is the 6,000 horsepower engine; neither GE or EMD have one in production yet. In the meantime, the Class I railroads are buying locomotives that can be upgraded to 6,000 horsepower later and that can use 4,300 (EMD) or 4,400 (GE) horsepower engines in the meantime.

SD80MAC

The SD80MAC is a 5,000 horsepower unit built around a 20-cylinder version of the tried-and-true 710 engine. It has all the new computer technology of the even more radical SD90MAC, but with an engine design that is a safer bet than the newer, more powerful "H" engine destined for the SD90MAC.

The SD80MAC is rated at 185,000 pounds starting effort, 147,000 continuous, both figures a gain of 10,000 pounds over the SD70MACs. Dynamic brake effort is 96,000 pounds. Adhesion is rated at an amazing 35 percent.

Fuel capacity is up to 5,800 gallons and oil up to 510 gallons, both substantially more than the SD70MAC.

The SD80MAC is 80 feet 2 inches long, 15 feet 8 inches high, and 10 feet 3 inches across the beam and weighs 415,000 pounds.

SD90MAC

The SD90MAC uses all the same basic components as the SD80MAC but with a new, 16-cylinder engine simply called the "H" that is scheduled for availability in 1997. This four-stroke engine is a first for EMD whose locomotives have always used two-stroke designs. At this writing, that's all EMD is saying.

Well, actually, they *did* say that with the 6,000 horsepower engine the SD90MAC will start getting close to pulling the couplers off the trailing load with 200,000 of *rated* starting tractive power; the SD70MAC has far exceeded its rated figures in real-world operations and if this model does as well somebody will be replacing a lot of coupler knuckles. Continuous tractive effort is 170,000 pounds and dynamic braking is up to 115,000 pounds. EMD claims a 40 percent adhesion rating and a maximum speed of 75 miles per hour.

Basic dimensions are identical to the SD80MAC. Capacity specifications, other than 5,800 gallons of fuel, aren't available at this writing.

AC6000

GE's new AC6000 uses an even bigger frame than the already huge 4400. That greater size is needed to accommodate a larger engine; it is also intended to permit greater cooling capacity. This brings the AC6000 to a length of 74 feet, the longest unit that GE could fit in the factory shops. GE has built 35 "convertibles" for Union Pacific with FDL engines that will be swaped out for the big Duetz engine when it is available.

The GE will introduce a totally new technology for linking the computer controls and all the components on the locomotive. GE isn't saying any more about it at this writing, but their promise is that the amount of control will be tremendously enhanced.

The AC6000 will provide 180,000 pounds of starting effort, 166,000 continuous, and offers 37 percent adhesion. Like the others, it is good for 75 miles per hour max. Fuel capacity is 5,900 gallons.

The Future

When asked to predict what's next for diesel locomotives, Sean responded, "Nobody knows. Six-thousand horsepower seems to be the limit for the available engines, for the foreseeable future. In fact, both builders are still trying to make these power plants work and neither are really ready for service. It will take a few years to work the kinks out of this new technology, and that's important to remember. There will be problems with these new engines—not just the technology of the locomotives themselves, but how the railroads use them in day-to-day operations. We are entering a period of adaptation."

continued on page 46

General Electric's latest and greatest is the AC6000CW. The new locomotive is equipped with a massive engine bay that will house a 6,000-horsepower powerplant. The Duetz engine will produce 180,000 pounds of starting effort and a continuous adhesion of 39 percent and uses 6-GEB13B traction motors. *Photo courtesy of General Electric*

continued from page 45

Dynamic brakes on the new units are one of the most important, and often overlooked, improved capabilities introduced with these locomotives. AC technology permits the use of dynamic brakes down to 0.2 miles per hour, a virtual standstill. That is really important in the mountains. "You can stop your train on a mountain grade with dynamic brakes alone," Sean says. "That saves your air for later, and engineers love this because it makes control so much better in the mountains. As important as AC is going uphill, it is just as important braking on the down slope. You don't overheat your traction motors with AC dynamic braking, a feature nobody usually mentions, but with the computer controls this makes control much better, safer, and saves wear on the brake components…yet another feature that makes accountants happy."

By the year 2000, hundreds of these 6,000-horsepower beasts will have revolutionized the North American railroad industry. Not only will the head end of trains look different, but the back end of the balance sheets will show a gain as well. In the meantime, the future of American railroads is rolling down the tracks today.

continued from page 43

The Universal line was typical of the design concepts of the second major phase of locomotive development, the period during the 1960s and 1970s when mechanical controls and hard-wired electrical systems were considered state-of-the-art. While these mechanical systems seem basic and primitive today, they were solid performers—powerful, reliable, maintainable. And a lot of train crews today like them a lot better than they do the new computer-controlled locomotives.

Dash 7

The long evolution of GE's second-generation locomotive family concluded with a U-boat with a curious name, the Dash 7. The proper name for the most common version of the Dash 7 locomotive was C30-7, and the -7 was in honor of nothing more significant than the year it was born, 1977. The C30-7 is a U30C in drag, with new makeup and a few fashionable accessories, but with the same old chassis and foundation: the same FDL 16-cylinder engine, same 3,000 horsepower, same frame, and same basic electrical systems, and with six powered axles on the C30 compared to the four on the U30B. General Electric also built Dash 7s with the smaller, 2,300-horsepower 12-cylinder engine or with the larger, 3,600-horsepower 16-cylinder engine. Depending on gearing, horsepower, and number of traction motors, a typical Dash 7 could pull at the draw bar with around 60,000 to 90,000 pounds of force.

The changes in the Dash 7 were numerous, extensive, and incremental rather than revolutionary—a response to an upgrade program based on the suggestions of 15 fleet operators. The Dash 7 was, and still is, a commercial success. Stand beside any track in the United States and a string of Dash 7s will likely soon thunder past. General Electric sold over a thousand of the six-axle U30C and C30-7 variants between 1967 and 1985, plus lots of others—some tricked out with cowl-bodied passenger locomotives

(U30CG and P30CH), a few with 12-cylinder 3,000-horsepower engines. The engineers were in what might be called "hogger" heaven with GE's Dash 7 . . . and then the Dash 8 came rolling down the track.

Dash 8

Then, in the early 1980s, GE introduced a diesel-electric with real improvements, this one called the Dash 8, allegedly in honor of the decade rather than anything logical. The Dash 8 not only introduced microprocessor control to the engine and traction control systems (with huge improvements in performance) but also initiated a new and even more illogical system of model description.

In many ways, the Dash 8 is the first of the really modern diesel locomotives. With it, GE started applying space-age computer-control technology to diesel-electric locomotives. It has been spectacularly successful, with over a thousand of the units sold in the first five years and was instrumental in making GE the leading North American manufacturer of locomotives, finally edging out EMD.

It's a *really* big unit, almost 71 feet long and better than 15 feet high; fully fueled (and with the crew full of lunch) it can weigh over 400,000 pounds. Everything about it is big: the fuel tank takes 5,000 gallons of number-two diesel fuel, an oil change (a rare event) needs 1,640 quarts, and the cooling system needs 380 gallons of coolant. The unit also carries 48 cubic feet of clean, dry sand for improving wheel to rail adhesion on slippery or wet rail.

It uses the same type of DC traction-motor technology that has powered diesel-electric locomotives since 1924—actually, the same motor design used for almost a hundred years—and with good reason: it works. The Dash 8 takes DC locomotive power to near its practical limits, providing almost 110,000 pounds of continuous tractive force, 149,000

Just about the time the folks at EMD were popping the champagne corks to celebrate their wonderful new SD70MAC, GE rolled out the AC4400 and ruined the party. The AC4400 is also an AC locomotive, but it outclasses the MAC in every way, including sales.

pounds starting tractive effort, and offering far better adhesion (up to 28 percent of axle weight) than was possible in the past. It is rated to a maximum speed of 70 miles per hour, and a minimum speed of 11 miles per hour—both good figures for traditional DC main-line freight locomotives.

Like nearly all the others in its old and numerous clan, the Dash 8 was built around the tried-and-true FDL-16 engine design GE has been using for decades. The variant of this engine used in the Dash 8 has been pumped up to 4,135 horsepower, mostly through turbocharging and computer-controlled fuel delivery.

The FDL-16 is a four-stroke diesel powerplant similar in concept to the engines used in trucks and some cars, with a power stroke alternating with an exhaust stroke every time the piston rises in the cylinder. This is a very different system than used on GM engines, a two-stroke-cycle design; although each is based on a different design concept, both do the same essential job with about the same efficiency and economy.

The FDL design has been around for many years and the version in the Dash 8 is not much dif-

ferent. The bore is a gaping 9 inches across, and the piston stroke is 10.5 inches. Compression is pretty typical of big diesels, about 13:1. A turbocharger boosts inlet air pressure, improving sea-level horsepower and eliminating the severe power loss suffered by normally aspirated engines (a loss of about 4 percent per 1,000 feet) at high altitude.

The engine drives a GE GMG187 DC generator wired to six GE752 traction motors. Computers within the control system of the locomotive can detect wheel slip and adjust the amount of power applied to the traction motor driving the axle, slowing it momentarily until slippage stops. That kind of wheel-slip control is standard now, but the Dash 8 was one of the very first to demonstrate how well computers can improve the performance of diesel-electric locomotives.

Dash 9

"As far as General Electric products, the Dash 9 is probably tops in DC locomotives," said one engineer who has tried them all. The Dash 9 is the current state-of-the-art in DC traction technology, the old U-Boat on steroids. The only locomotive specification that really means anything—tractive effort—is 140,000 pounds for the Dash 9 when starting, 109,000 pounds continuous! That is roughly *double* the go-power of equivalent locomotives of the recent past

Dash 9 Specs & Performance
Diesel Engine Power: 4,000–4,400 horsepower
Tractive Effort (continuous): 109,000 pounds
Tractive Effort (starting): 140,000 pounds
Adhesion: 28 percent
Dynamic Brake: 78,000 pounds
Fuel Capacity: 5,000 gallons
Engine: 7FDL, 16 cylinders, electronic fuel injection

Wheels: 40 inches
Trucks: GE HiAd (high adhesion) Low Weight
Maximum Speed: 70 miles per hour

AC4400CW

General Electric's entry into the AC traction market came several months after the SD70MAC, with improved performance specifications and sales. While Burlington Northern made a large buy of the EMD locomotive, many more railroads have selected the AC4400CW. The GE machine has more tractive force and more dynamic brake effort,—all in a package that costs about the same to acquire and operate. You'll find hundreds running for the CSX, Southern Pacific, Union Pacific, and Canadian Pacific.

As one engineer said, "The AC4400CWs are very different locomotives—very powerful, with some quirks. With a conventional locomotive running light you can sometimes start out by putting the throttle up in Notch 3 or 4, start moving, then add another notch or two. Try that with the new ACs and they will jump and buck like they're coming off the rails! They are *very* fast, and the dynamic brakes are phenomenal."

Canadian National 5610 is an SD70 I, a variant of the SD70 common to that railroad. Canadian National introduced the Canadian cab over 20 years ago, in 1973, and continues to refine the concept. Canadian National 5610 is poised to depart the Belt Railway of Chicago's Clearing Yard at Bedford Park, Illinois, on a cold, crisp Christmas Day 1995. *Sean Graham-White*

AC4400CW Specs & Performance

Diesel Engine Power: 4,400 horsepower
Tractive Effort (continuous): 145,000 pounds
Tractive Effort (starting): 180,000 pounds
Adhesion: 35 percent
Dynamic Brake: 98,000 pounds
Fuel Capacity: 5,000 gallons
Engine: 7FDL, 16 cylinders, electronic fuel injection
Wheels: 42 inches
Trucks: GE HiAd (high adhesion) Low Weight
Maximum Speed: 75 miles per hour

CHAPTER THREE

Anatomy of a Locomotive

Locomotive anatomy is essentially the same today as when the general layout was developed 70 years ago. The most modern AC4400CWs and SD70MACs use engines, motors, trucks, compressors, and many of the accessory components pretty much in the same spot on the frame as did the earliest models. While this makes it fairly easy to recognize individual components on all locomotives, it makes recognition of specific models extremely difficult without a guidebook.

It's 0400 hours at Kansas City's locomotive hospital; Santa Fe's Argentine shops repair every locomotive in the fleet—three shifts, seven days a week. The locomotives don't stay long—a few hours or a day or two; then they're back on the rails, working for a living.

51

Some aspects of locomotive design philosophy are quite different from other vehicles and take a little getting used to—vehicle weight, for example. In just about every other machine that rolls or flies or floats, weight is a negative factor, a penalty. Weight is a virtue on a locomotive, though, and ballast is commonly added during the design process. That's because the locomotive's ability to pull a load (tractive force) is directly related to the weight on the driving wheels before the wheels start to slip. A conventional DC locomotive's wheels start to slip when the drawbar pull equals about 20 percent of the locomotive's weight; the new AC locomotives keep pulling up to about 45 percent of total weight on the wheels. So many of the compo-

Major repairs on the Santa Fe go to Topeka, Kansas, where the heavy repair and overhaul work is done. The shop has opened up a GP60M, exposing the big 16-cylinder diesel engine and some of the accessories. The technician is working on the big generator, just back of the electrical panel up near the cab.

right
A Dash 9 slides out of the yard, eastbound. Access to the wide cabs is through a nose door, thoughtfully left open by the crew to provide a little forced-air ventilation. Directly behind the cab on this model are the dynamic brake cooling air inlets; the exhausts are on the top surface. Access to the many electrical systems is provided by the panels visible on the left side.

left
The brushes on conventional DC generators are huge. They are also a source of fairly frequent service problems, one reason for the trend toward AC technology (which doesn't use brushes).

below
Every half-million miles or so the engines of most Santa Fe locomotives come back to Topeka for complete rebuilds. This block already has the crank reinstalled, and the mechanics are finishing up that phase of the work by replacing the bearing caps, complete with fresh inserts.

The design of the cabs on all modern locomotives anticipates collisions with cars and trucks, something that happens with surprising frequency. This F40 has just survived an encounter with a truck; the truck was demolished but the locomotive just needs a little body and fender work. Pass the Bondo!

nents of a locomotive are intentionally massive, beginning with the frame.

Frame

Underneath the sheet metal and paint, normally invisible, the frame of the locomotive is a stunningly massive component. Frames are either fabricated, welded from steel bars up to four inches thick, or cast. In either case they are huge, often over 50 feet long, and extremely strong.

That strength is necessary for three basic reasons: first, to support the engine, generator or alternator, and other components; second, to toler-

ate the tremendous forces from the draw bar when pulling a train; third, to protect the crew in a crash. But extra steel or even concrete is often added, far beyond the requirements of these functions, just to increase weight, thereby improving adhesion. Some early locomotives had to be scrapped before their major systems were quite worn out when the frames developed irreparable cracks from the stresses and strains of work on the railroad.

Cab and Hood

The sheet-metal portion of a locomotive is another area of extreme standardiza-

This lady is releasing the hand brake on this EMD SD45 before hooking it up as part of a consist. The radiator air inlet is above her head, slanted outward; the radiator itself is on the top of the locomotive, vented by three large fans. In the middle of the long hood section, also tilted outward, is the dynamic-brake or "retarder" grids. The EMD locomotives tend to be quite slab-sided, a recognition feature.

tion. While there are obvious differences in the appearance of the locomotives you'll see in the yards and on the main line, don't expect to use cab shape, for example, to identify a specific model. There are over 10 tiny variants to cab design and you will find

them on dozens of models, and it takes lots of experience to use them to identify one model from another.

The hood itself is laced with access doors, air inlets, and exhaust vents. Despite the dozens of models, it is fairly easy to recognize the functions of the intakes and exhausts—once you know what goes where (see illustration) on a given locomotive type. Behind the cab, for instance, are the following common features:

Dynamic-brake bulges at the top of the hood (first and second generation EMD). These bulges, often with a distinctive shape usually in the middle of the locomotive, house the dynamic-brake resistor grids on most older models. Newer Dash 8s and SDs have the internal resistor grinds moved forward behind the cab, with intakes on the side of the locomotive and exhaust vents on top. Not all locomotives are equipped with dynamic brakes, but they are easy to spot on EMD products: They are always in the middle of the hood on first- and second-generation EMD (third-generation GPs) and always directly behind the cab on third-generation SDs (see photo).

Engine air intakes toward the front of the engine on both GE and EMD locomotives.

Turbocharger (if turbocharged) exhausts—usually a boxy, square tube—projecting from the top of the hood, about six inches above the sheet metal. On EMD locomotives, this exhaust is located towards the front of the unit; on GE locomotives, the exhaust is located farther aft, near the locomotive's radiator section. All GE locomotives

The radiator area of a GE AC4400. The GE locomotives almost always have "gull-wing" radiator extensions, another recognition feature.

The electrical shop at Topeka rebuilds traction motors by the thousands and generators by the hundreds. Here's a rotor being checked for run-out after a major overhaul.

are turbocharged, but not all EMDs are. Several classes of EMD locomotives are fed air by a roots-type supercharger and not by a turbo-supercharger. Supercharged locomotives will generally have two or four exhaust stacks centered down the spine of the locomotive. These are often located on either side of the dynamic-brake fan. It is interesting to note that on EMD locomotives the turbocharger is actually driven by a clutch mechanism off the engine (prime mover) at low rpms when there is insufficient exhaust-gas pressure to spin the turbine. This clutch mechanism releases when the exhaust-gas pressure passes a point that is sufficient to spin the turbine without the help of the prime mover. Hence the description "turbo-

supercharger." GE locomotives do not use this clutch mechanism; this is what causes the turbo-lag (dark black exhaust when throttling up) common to GE locomotives. This dark black exhaust is actually caused by air starvation of the engine, but this condition is quickly corrected by increased rpm and thus increased turbine speed feeding the GE engine with sufficient air for clean combustion.

An engine-coolant radiator on the roof line or at the top rear. The radiator is invariably at the top rear on GE locomotives. It is often identified by the flared projections and by air-intake vents along the sides of the hood towards the rear of the unit. First-generation EMD locomotives (GP7 through the GP20) split their radiator

Fred Cash came to work for Southern Pacific during the days of steam. He'll tell you that replacing a piston is a *lot* easier now! He's in the process of reinstalling a power pack or complete cylinder assembly in a SD45T-2, a three-hour job if everything goes right.

sections into two locations along the roof line: one in front of the prime mover and the other aft of the prime mover. Second-generation EMD locomotives (GP30 forward) have two or three round fans and their associated intake grills located towards the rear of the locomotive's long hood. Both GE and EMD locomotives have large screened intakes located just below the radiators for cooling air. The GE locomotives have historically drawn their cooling air from low on the locomotive car body. The EMD locomotives inhale their air from intakes mounted along the sides of the top of the hood. This arrangement has proven to be less than favorable when multiple locomotives are pulling heavy trains up a

steep grade and pass through a long tunnel. The lead units tend to super-heat the air high within the tunnel, thus decreasing the ability for the rear units to cool themselves. This, of course, causes the following locomotives' engines to shut down because of overheating, which is not desirable on a long ascending grade. To counter this EMD-only problem, the "tunnel motor" was invented for and used extensively by Southern Pacific and Rio Grande. The SD40T-2s and SD45T-2s have a modified rear radiator section (looking much like the GE radiator section, minus the flares). These intakes draw cool, breathable air up from the floor of the tunnel, thus providing more cooling capability in tunnels.

The distinctive blister amidships on nearly all EMD locomotives houses the dynamic-brake grids; with the retarder engaged, momentum is converted to electricity, and the electricity is converted to heat; the heat is then vented through this housing.

Conventional Cab

The conventional cab, found in many variations, has a boxy style that is gradually disappearing. It is a relic of the older EMD and GE designs of the 1950s, 1960s, 1970s and 1980s. Visibility is much better on these older cabs than in the newer cabs, but the lack of a nose protecting the entire width of the cab front increases the risk of cab damage in the event of a collision. Vision from both the standard narrow-nose cabs and the newer wide-nose cabs is identical and severely limited when the long end is forward as was once standard operating procedure on the Southern and Norfolk Western railroads, now Norfolk Southern. These railroads operated their locomotives long hood forward to protect the cab in the

Modular electronics started appearing on locomotives in the 1960s, a radical improvement over the old hard-wired technology.

This AC4400 is nearly new but it has already been involved in a grade-crossing incident. The paint scrapes and broken glass are from a Volkswagen that tried to beat the train, and lost. That large hose is for the main train-line air brakes. The other three hoses control the independent air brakes and sanders on the locomotives in the consist.

event of a collision. Entry to the cab is provided by two doors, one forward and one aft, on both wide-nose and standard cabs.

The rear wall of the cab interior contains the electrical cabinet. Some of the instrumentation and controls are on this rear wall. This console contains the many relays and circuits for locomotive control, transitioning, reversing, dynamic braking, and so on. This plethora of wiring is accessible to the crews and shop personnel via access doors on the back cab wall.

Canadian Cab (Wide Nose)

The cab layout most modern in appearance is the full-cab-width nose design called the "Canadian," "Comfort," or "Safety" cab—a rather handsome style remotely similar to the DDA40X cabs that were built in 1969. These wide-nose cabs were originally designed to provide an extra margin of protection for the crew when a collision occurs, plus to provide some additional crew comforts. The first wide-nose locomotives (GP38-2Ws, GP40-2Ws, SD40-2Ws) were custom units built by EMD and delivered to

Pneumatic and electrical connections make multiple locomotives function as one. Spare coupler knuckles are visible on both locomotives, ready to replace the ones that inevitably break—even though they're rated to 500,000 pounds.

the Canadian National in the early 1970s. General Electric also produced some custom cabs, the rather odd-looking BQ23-7, which was delivered to the Family Lines in the late 1970s. Both EMD and GE started offering the wide nose as an option, rather than as special order, in 1988.

Both EMD and GE build variants of the Canadian cab. Although the cab appears to be fabricated from thin sheet metal similar to that used for automobile and truck bodies, these Canadian cabs use heavy steel plate similar to that used on some armored combat vehicles. This steel, typically about 1/8 inch thick, will shrug off an encounter with an automobile with little more than scratched paint. And the design

of the surfaces are—just as with a tank—intended to deflect an impact away from the cab and its occupants. This armor plate is always further reinforced inside the cab with massive vertical steel members, further protecting the cab's occupants from heavier objects (like the occasional semi or logging truck or, more commonly, another train).

The difference between the old-style conventional cab and the newer Canadian style goes far beyond the sheet metal. Despite its function as an armored cupola for the crew, the Canadian cab is occasionally isolated from the frame, attached securely but insulated from the noise and vibration of the frame and body.

This "WhisperCab" is separated from the frame with a large rubber "doughnut" that absorbs much of the rattles and bangs that make conventional cabs so noisy that hearing protection is often required.

The layout and design of the engineer's controls and instrumentation is also quite different in the conventional and Canadian cabs—the latter often incorporating computer-controlled instrumentation based on the same "glass-cockpit" philosophy used in contemporary fighter aircraft such as the F-15E and F/A-18. Oddly enough, there is better visibility from the older conventional cabs. Conventional cabs use a control stand on the engineer's left and front, cluttered with controls, switches, circuit breakers, and instruments; new locomotives use one or more multi-function displays (MFDs) that display information selected by the engineer and a much-simplified set of controls. While these new layouts look impressive, the crews are not always pleased with the new control configuration, partly because of the way you have to sit to operate them—arms straight ahead, eyes forward, too—and partly because the controls are set up quite differently.

Mel Wilson, an engineer with experience in many kinds of locomotives, said, "Somebody thinks we all enjoy the desktop controls on the new locomotives—you read about how great they are—but we don't like them. In fact, Norfolk Southern is buying new SD70s and Dash 9s with the old conventional cabs, and I wish we would do the same. The Dash 9 is mechanically one of the best locomotives on the road—to have one with the old control stand would be wonderful! The standard cab has a better layout for actually running the train. You can watch what's happening outside much better, and the controls are placed more comfortably within natural reach."

The EMD version was introduced in 1973 for Canadian National, but it wasn't until 1988 that its use spread across North America. Since then, its popularity has grown quickly and it can be found on almost every six-axle locomotvie EMD turns out.

The first optional—as opposed to custom—Canadian cab from GE was offered on a B40-8W in 1988 and has since become commonplace on the six-axle Dash 8, Dash 9, and AC lines—but you will still see some with conventional cabs. Ironically, for both builders, the Canadian cab is now standard on six-axle locomotives.

While the layout and setup of these modern cabs varies considerably, the lower noise and vibration, the luxury of air conditioning in many cabs, and the increased crew protection all make for greater comfort for the engineer and conductor responsible for these expensive machines.

Fuel Tank

Suspended under the frame and often occupying the space between the forward and rear truck assemblies is the fuel tank. The capacity of this tank on modern locomotives is often 5,000 gallons. Why so much fuel when service facilities are only a couple of hundred miles

A fresh wheel and axle, ready for installation.

These truck assemblies are GE's HiAd (high adhesion) Low Weight design, installed on the 4400 and the Dash 9.

apart? Even with the engine gulping two gallons to the mile, one fill-up will take you across the United States. The answer: The fuel adds weight to the locomotive, improving adhesion.

Couplers

The Janney Coupler, invented back in the 1880s and standard across the United States, Canada, and Mexico for many years, is a rather ingenious device. For all its cast-iron bulk, it is still the intentional weak link that connects the engines and the cars that form a train. The forces on the coupler can be amazing; a typical 100-car train running on dead-level track will exert a resistance on that first coupler of the trailing load of about 50,000 pounds. But track is seldom level, and the forces on the coupler are often far higher. The principal factor limiting the size of trains is the rated strength of couplers, nominally 250,000 pounds.

By Federal Railroad Administration regulation, the top of the coupler knuckle must be between 31.5 inches and 34.5 inches above the top of the rail, a dimension that gets checked after the locomotive's wheels are turned; it is possible to alter coupler height, particularly if only one set of drive wheels gets turned. The most common cause of coupler height shift is the natural compression of the locomotive springs caused by their eventual loss of elasticity. This problem is corrected by re-springing the locomotive and by shimming the coupler periodically.

Engine and Drivetrain

The drive wheels of modern diesel-electric locomotives are driven in basically the same fashion as were the electric locomotives of a hundred years ago: They are driven by large electric traction motors. The difference is that diesel-electrics do not have to rely on getting their electric power from an outside power cable; instead, they carry huge diesel engines that are hooked up to massive generators (DC) or alternators (AC) that supply the electricity for the traction motors. In effect, the huge diesel engines carried by these locomotives are little more than gargantuan versions of those little gas-powered portable generators that are so common today.

Engine Block

Locomotive engine blocks are not the biggest of the breed—those on ships are much larger—but they still seem immense. A typical block, a 16-cylinder model, will be roughly 9 feet high by 5 feet wide by 15 feet long. There are two ways to make these blocks: casting and fabrication.

Railroads keep these components working for decades, rebuilding them during major overhauls every 600,000 to a million miles or so. Santa Fe's Topeka shops overhaul these engines constantly, stripping them, running the components through an acid bath, inspecting and refurbishing all the major and minor components, then reassembling the whole package. These rebuilt "long-block" engines are kept ready to install in Santa Fe's massive fleet of locomotives when an engine has a catastrophic failure or is worn enough to need a rebuild.

Power Assemblies

Individual cylinders on locomotive engines are separate assemblies, called "power assemblies," designed for easy removal and replacement. That means the cylinder head is an integral component of the individual cylinder, rather than a shared component as with the heads on truck and automobile engines. With typical displacement of individual cylinders running about 600 to 700 cubic inches—far more than that of the entire engine of a full-sized automobile—everything about these components is big. A bare connecting rod weighs about 25 pounds. A piston is about 9 inches across, and with a stroke of 10 or 11 inches, the bore of the cylinder liner looks like a bottomless pit.

Four-cycle diesel engines are standard on GE locomotives and use intake and exhaust valves and an overhead-cam system similar to that of a truck diesel engine; the cam shaft, though, is off to the side of the cylinder head to allow easy removal of the power pack from the block. The EMD locomotives have traditionally used two-cycle engines, a design that forfeits a little fuel efficiency in favor of a simplified design. The two-stroke engine doesn't use a cam shaft or valves at all—the piston also controls the intake of air and the exhaust of the burned fuel mixture by exposing the exhaust/intake ports as it nears the bottom of its travel at the end of each downward stroke.

When a cylinder fails and needs replacement, the shop mechanics first disconnect the upper fittings of the assembly—retainers, fuel line, and valve lifters on some models, about a 15-minute job if all goes well. Next, the lower part of the assembly—the connecting rod bolts and cap—is accessed through a panel in the block and disconnected, another 15 minutes under normal conditions. Then, the power assembly is lifted out with the help of a crane and a special bracket. A new power assembly from on-site storage (complete with new or

reconditioned piston, connecting rod, bearings, rings, valves, and other components) is lifted into place; this takes at least two mechanics, and special care is taken to keep the edges of the connecting-rod bearing cap from scratching the polished surface of the crank shaft as the assembly is lowered into the block. When the fasteners are torqued and inspected and all the covers are refastened, the engine is "good to go."

Trucks

The traction-wheel motor-truck assembly is the key to the performance of the locomotive, and a tremendous amount of engineering time and talent was invested in these heavy, often grimy components under the frame. That's because the design of the trucks has a lot to do with how well the engine's power can be transmitted to the rail and how comfortably the locomotive rides.

Despite appearances, the locomotive doesn't ride directly on the heavy cast-steel frame above the wheels, but on an intermediate assembly attached to the frame—the bolster. The suspension design varies but always involves some kind of springing between the bolster and the wheels to dampen both vertical and lateral shocks. This springing can be in the form of leaf or coil springs or rubber pads. On some designs, springs are supported by "swing hangers" that permit about 2.5 inches of lateral travel, smoothing the ride when a locomotive enters a curve at speed.

Two- and three-axle trucks are the standard today, each axle typically applying about 70,000 pounds of the locomotive's weight to the rail. Union Pacific's big EMD *Centennial* DD40AX, has four driven axles on each truck, a total of eight, and more (and less) could theoretically be used.

Regardless of the number of axles and traction motors, the power output of the engine is divided equally among them; both two and three axle trucks have operational virtues and vices.

The truck assembly includes the wheels and axles (one solid component), with a traction motor attached to each axle. These in turn are part of the truck frame assembly, a large cast steel component. The frame is attached to the bolster with a suspension—springs, pads, swing hangers, or a combination that smooths the ride. The bolster itself attaches to the frame of the locomotive, held in place only by gravity. Massive electrical cables provide power to the traction motors and an air line serves the brakes.

Locomotive wheels vary in diameter, with 40-inch and 42-inch wheels typical on the most modern locomotives such as the SD70 and Dash 9. Wheels and axles are massive components, applying all that horsepower to the rail. While early diesel locomotives sometimes incorporated unpowered axles, all contemporary models use traction motors on each axle.

Brakes

Locomotives can have three sets of brakes, each usable individually or in concert—and they can stop the locomotive relatively quickly, especially when you consider how much weight they must bring to a halt, provided the engineer does not apply excessive braking effort, causing the locomotive's wheels to slide.

The first set of brakes is the independent brakes, a set of air-actuated brakes that act on all the wheels of the locomotive. The independent brakes work much like the brakes on your automobile, except that these are pneumatically actuated instead of hydraulically actuated. Replacing these brake shoes is one of the most common maintenance chores on locomotives.

The second set is the dynamic brakes, which use the traction motors to apply braking force to the drive wheels. Not every locomotive is equipped with dynamic brakes, but they are extremely common, particularly on locomotives used to negotiate long grades. When applied, the dynamic brakes turn the traction motors into generators, the speed and momentum of the train acting against the resistance of the magnetic fields; it takes work to generate electricity and that work slows the train. The electricity is converted to heat in large toaster-like grids and is blown out vents at the top of the hood. Dynamic brakes are essential for train management on the steep grades common on many railroads throughout the world. Dynamic brakes actually supplement, rather than replace, the independent brakes and the train brake system. Typically, the dynamic bakes are most effective at around 10 to 25 miles per hour.

The third set is the "train-line" air brakes, a system invented by George Westinghouse over a century ago—and still the most practical way to safely control the speed of a long, heavy train. This system is also pneumatically actuated, but it is hooked up to each wheel in each car in the train, spreading the braking force out over many wheels and brake shoes. The shoes on each car release when the train-line "pipe" is pressurized with air supplied by large tanks on the locomotives. A large chunk of the power of the diesel engine goes to drive a huge air compressor that keeps these tanks charged. No train in North America moves until this system is visually checked with an air-brake test.

Traction Motors

Though diesel-electric locomotives have huge diesel engines, it is the electric-powered traction motors that actually put the power to the

Ooops, I think we better shut down this engine. Actually, the engine shut itself down with a bang when the crankshaft failed. Those are bits and pieces of the connecting rod, piston, and bearing cap in the background. The crank is beyond help but the block will be rebuilt.

right
You've just about got to be a contortionist to work on the air conditioner on Dash 8s, but it is in there somewhere. Although the power of new locomotives is much improved, the people who work on them object to the growing complexity and inaccessibility of many components.

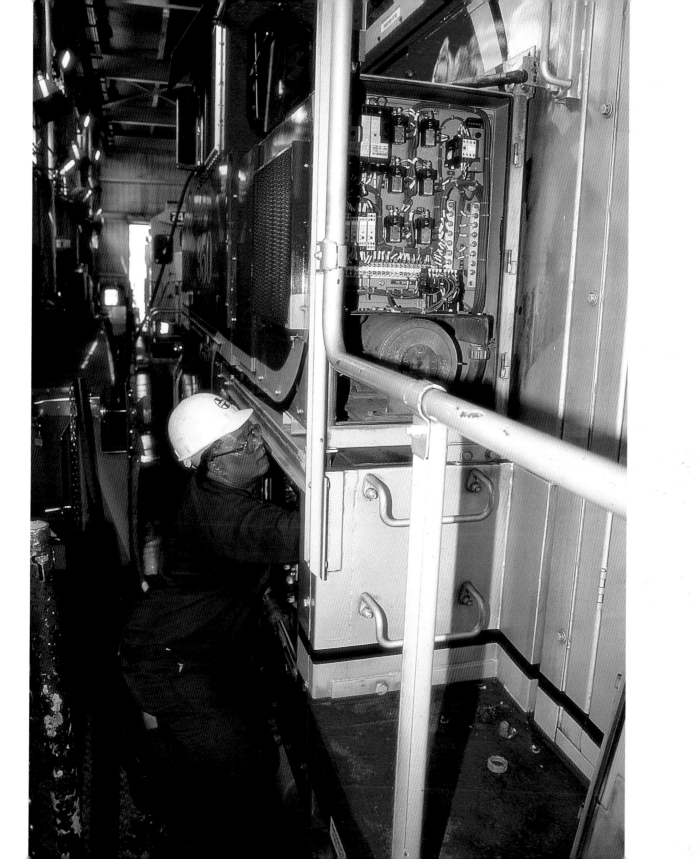

The fuel tank on an AC4400 holds 5,000 gallons. The two smaller cylinders are the air tanks for the train-line air brakes.

rail. Traction motors are large and extremely powerful electric motors, able to produce tremendous torque. There are two types, the traditional DC design, standard for a hundred years, and the new AC types. The exciting thing about AC traction motor technology is that it improves adhesion under difficult conditions. The use of AC traction motors and their associated computer control systems has revolutionized the power on the point of certain kinds of trains, particularly those used on the heavy coal hauls from the Powder River Basin in Wyoming and in the mountains of Colorado. As a result of improved traction on AC locomotives railroads are using fewer locomotives for the same size trains as before.

North American locomotives mount the traction motors in a somewhat different way from those in Europe and elsewhere. The motors are supported by the axle on one side, which allows them to pivot in response to irregularities in the track. The other side of the motor rests on pads on the truck frame.

"Because of the smooth steel wheels and rails, it can be very difficult to get a train started—particularly if there is even a tiny amount of oil or ice on the tracks," reported Jeff Garrett, Amtrak engineer. "When that happens, it takes a long time to get up to your maximum speed. Sand helps, and it can be applied to the rail head automatically or manually, depending on what's happening."

70

"On the older locomotives you used to be able to start a train by jamming the throttle from Idle all the way up to run 8; 1,500 amps went to the traction motors and the wheels would spin and slip like crazy. Now, though, traction is controlled by computer. Each individual axle is monitored; when one starts to slip power is reduced to that traction motor until the slippage stops."

Passenger versus Freight Locomotives

The difference between locomotives designed for passenger use and for freight-train use is more substantial than the cowl bodies and pretty paint jobs common to CalTrain, Amtrak, Metro, and the commuter lines of the East Coast. A freight train typically weighs 7,000 tons or more—a passenger train only 800 tons. A freight locomotive needs tremendous power for pulling heavy loads, usually at moderate speeds; a passenger locomotive has to be able to sprint from a standing start to high speed, and to come to a halt, with elegant smoothness. A passenger locomotive also needs to provide electrical power for light and heating or air conditioning for the entire train it is pulling.

F59PHI: The California Bullet Train

The EMD California Locomotive, the F59PHI used by CalTrans (California Department of Transportation) for Amtrak and a growing number of other lines, is pretty typical of the modern breed of passenger power. The F stands for "fully cowled," an aerodynamic body style that cuts air drag at speed; the 59 is a model sequence number; P is for "passenger"; H for (hotel) head-end power—an additional diesel engine and electrical generator to supply power for the passenger cars; and I for "isolated" cab. The engine has only 12 cylinders, not the 16 used on most freight locomotives.

"The cab is rather tiny," Jeff Garrett said, "but they are very quiet compared to the F40s, and they ride better, too. They are quite good mechanically, but everything is computerized. I was running 2003 today, and it decided to shut itself down for low oil quantity. Well, that's fine except that with the older models you could go back and check the dipstick—if the quantity was okay you could reset the alarm, and off you'd go. Not anymore! You can't trouble-shoot anymore, and if the computer says you can't move, you don't move! "

cHApTER four

The View from the Cab

There are two ways you can look at a locomotive—from the outside, standing by the track, or from the inside with the train crew. Well, the railroads are pretty stingy about having sight-seers cluttering up the cab but— through the magic of literature—Motorbooks has arranged for you to get a guided tour of several types of modern diesel locomotives, complete with the insights and perspectives of the "hoggers" who actually operate them. What is it like to sit in the right seat of a lash-up of those big, glittering modern SD70MACs or Dash 9s, or even the older SD40-2s or C30-7s?

Canadian National 2101 and a long string of "oil cans" powers out of Hamilton, Ontario. This locomotive is a product of Bombardier, a Canadian company that replaced Montreal Locomotive Works, the company that produced this HR616 model in 1982, then went out of the freight locomotive business in 1985. *Howard Ande*

"Running a train isn't so much watching dials or controls—it is *feeling* what's going on behind you," said Stephen Priest. You can sense how it is tugging at you, how much it is resisting the locomotive consist [a consist is a gang of several locomotives working together]. If it feels like there's a lot of resistance, you make sure you don't throttle up—you could possibly break your train in half. You become sensitized to minute changes in terrain or track alignment. Curves, for instance, will always slow you down."

"Now, what do you think would be easier to run—a long train or a short train? Surprisingly, it is the long train because it is spread out over a mile or more of terrain, and that tends to cancel out some of the forces that cause problems with short trains. Some of the train will be going uphill while another part will be going down; the result tends toward neutrality. A short train requires much more work by the engineer."

AC versus DC in the Cab

"The new AC locomotives have a lot of advantages," according to Stephen Priest. "The DC traction motor has a couple of problems for us; one, it has to go through a 'transition' phase as it goes faster and faster; this involves switching changes that basically 'rewire' the traction motor to avoid the increased internal resistance that occurs as it speeds up. The older locomotives typically go through a very rough transition. If you've got a hundred cars full of grain

Here's what you see from the hot-seat of the "plain vanilla" American locomotive, the SD45—and just about any other model with a conventional cab. This one is wound up and ready to go; the engineer is waiting for me to hurry up and get out of the way because he's got places to go. The two big dials report on air pressure for the train-line and independent brakes. Many engineers prefer this control stand to the new version; the controls are easier to reach—and you can put your feet up on the heater, below the window.

F40PH cab. Passenger locomotives get the same instrumentation as the freight models, plus some extras for the head-end power systems that provide heat and light for the passenger cars. This is a typical cockpit for a hard-working commuter locomotive. The radio is on the upper left, the air horn control next to it, and the brake has a bright orange handle. The throttle is fully forward, in the Idle position. A major improvement on the F40 is the foot rest in front of the heater outlet.

This is the cockpit of the first post-war six-axle freight design, the SD9. If you can run one of these, you won't have any trouble with a Dash 9 or AC4400, the engineers will tell you. During the process of starting a train, the engineer monitors that huge ammeter on top of the console, keeping the needle at about 1,000 amps.

and four older GEs, for example, you *pray* that the transition won't pull the train apart. It is *very* rough! You feel the traction motors cut out on you, then engage with a forward lurch that kicks you in the seat of the pants. The ACs are very different in the way they work; first, there isn't a transition phase, so acceleration is smooth and progressive. Second, they are spectacularly powerful! If I have four or five older SD40-2s, for example, and want to take off from a dead stop, I can advance the throttle to Run 4 or Run 5 and the locomotives will shudder a little and slowly start to move the train. If you go past Run 1 in one of the new ACs they will just about jump off the tracks! If you're used to the old power and get assigned to one of these things, you're accustomed to just knocking the throttle all the way out there—the locomotives will start surging up and down like a racehorse!"

F59PHI Cab Ride

Train crews don't have nine-to-five jobs or a fixed routine. They often work all hours of the day or night, on all kinds of equipment, to any destination on their division, in any kind of power available from an older SW1500 yard switcher to a new AC4400CW on a hot-shot freight. The pattern is a bit different for passenger-train engineers and crews—the same unpredictability about hours but usually on the same kind of locomotive and normally on the same run.

Jeff Garrett is an Amtrak engineer. He runs the new California version of the F59PHI locomotive, normally on the "Capitols" route between San Jose and Sacramento, California. His work day begins with a call and two-hour notification, just as do crews on freight trains. He checks in at the Amtrak office, signs the register, and receives track warrants and bulletins. These documents describe track conditions for Garrett's assigned run, a distance that may be about 100 to 250 miles. He can be assigned the

And here's the new look in cockpits, the "desktop" design. This version is aboard the F59PHI, engineer Jeff Garrett at the helm. The airline gauges are easily recognizable, and the throttle, directional control, dynamic brake, bell, sander, air horn, radio, and other systems are still available, but they've been moved around a bit. Many engineers dislike the posture required to use these controls—always faced forward, arms extended, with no place to prop your feet. The throttle is in idle here, but when moved to Run 8, full power, the train will accelerate at about one mile per hour per second—not bad for a single locomotive pulling 800 tons of train.

A conventional cab, such as the one on this Denver & Rio Grande Western GP40, allows you to work the locomotive in either direction, as this hostler (as a person who moves trains in the yard but not on the mainline is called) is doing in the Roseville Yard.

run from Oakland to Sacramento—or Lovelock, Nevada, or down to Santa Barbara, or anywhere within his 12-hour range on the Amtrak system.

Crew Brief

After he's had a chance to digest the track warrant and bulletins, it is time for the crew briefing. That's when the conductor, the assistant conductor (formerly known as the brakeman) and the engineer get together to discuss the trip—how many track maintenance gangs will be slowing them today and how many slow orders and special speed limits are in effect during this run.

The crew is transported from the office to the yard, where the train has already been assembled and the locomotives have been fully fueled, started, air brakes tested, and supplied by the mechanical department. Garrett backs the train down to the station—OKJ to the crews, Jack London Station on the time table—so that the locomotive is headed in the right direction, north, for the trip to Sacramento.

Once the train is spotted for loading, Garrett and the crew execute the air test required by Federal Railroad Administration regulations. While Jeff applies and releases the train

This engineer is watching the last passengers board Train 50 at one of the oldest passenger rail stations in the U.S., at Santa Clara, California , in the rear-view mirror; then he'll ring the bell, release the brakes, move the directional control to Forward, throttle to Run 1, and it is off to the next station, College Park.

brakes, the conductor and the assistant conductor inspect the brake shoes to ensure each responds. "Air test okay," the conductor reports on the radio, "Highball!"

Highball

The "highball" signal comes at 0715 hours, a green light ahead. "Clear block!" Garrett calls to Mike McBride, Garrett's Amtrak supervisor, along today for a routine familiarization run. "Green signal!" McBride responds. Garrett moves the reverser to Forward, independent brakes to Off, throttle from Idle to Run 1 . . . and away we go.

It's a bit noisy in the cab—you can hear the engine rev up, the blowers humming, the radio squawking; back in the passenger cars people read, chat, drink coffee. Amtrak 6 glides out of the station right on time, without a bump or a shiver to betray its movement.

A passenger train trip is a series of races from one station to the next. The opponent is the clock, and victory is won when the train arrives on time. Jeff accelerates Amtrak 6 up to 70 miles per hour, dashing quickly past the crossing gates, watching always for the idiot who drives around the gates or the pedestrian ambling across the tracks.

left
Running commuter trains such as this F40, roaring down the track at 70 miles per hour, is a very challenging, emotionally exhausting business. Nearly all the engineers on this 50-mile run, between San Jose and San Francisco, have had people die under their wheels—some are suicides, some run the crossing gates, some are trying to escape from the police, some are little children playing on the tracks. One engineer on this run has had 12 people die in front of him. It takes a lot of the fun out of the business of running trains.

Jeff, like most engineers, has had some awful experiences running trains. Once he clipped a truck with a large propane tank; the tank ruptured, filling the cab with an explosive mixture of gas and air. It didn't ignite or Jeff wouldn't be running 722.

"Fatal collisions are a fact of life for an engineer," Jeff says, "a part of the job. But you never forget it, either. You can almost see the event happen, over and over. It happens right in front of you, at very close range, and you don't forget it. My first one was very sad, a 23-year-old girl who dropped her father off at work and came roaring out of the parking lot without seeing me. She came right into the side of me, got dragged a ways—she was killed right in front of her father.

"The second was a car I hit broadside at sixty miles per hour—I was on the *California Zephyr*, coming up past another engine doing some switching work on a siding. This guy drove around all the other cars waiting at the gate, drove around the gate, and across the tracks—I could see him, he wasn't even looking! Bang! We dragged him half a mile, locked onto the drawbar. He was 23, too.

"When something like that happens, we hit the floor. You don't know what's going to happen with that car, it could come up and into the cab with you. You don't know if you're going to derail. You can smell all the gasoline from the car's tank…it is AWFUL. It happens

left
Even when your fuel tank holds thousands of gallons, you still need to pull over once in a while, check the oil, scrape the bugs off the windshield, and walk around. Periodic inspections of locomotives and trains are not only a good idea, daily inspections are required by the federal government.

very fast, in slow motion, and is very noisy. You don't get over it.

"Hitting a person is amazingly noisy. As big as a locomotive is, you hear any little thing you hit—it resonates throughout the cab. There is a real loud thud when you hit a person, and you can hear them being dragged under the engine. I had one guy in Reno stand on the tracks and let me clobber him—looked me right in the eye. Generally, when you're involved in a fatality, you don't get off the engine. You wait for the police to come; you don't go look at the body. Even so, I can conjure up each one in my mind. I've been involved in five of them. They don't go away."

Jeff will run 6 from Oakland up to Sparks, Nevada, watching the signals and the clock and the cars at the crossings. The F59PHI accelerates rapidly (for a locomotive) from each of the many stops along the way—Martinez, Vacaville, Davis, Sacramento, Auburn—on its journey eastbound. It roars across the great central valley of California, then up across 100 miles of rolling hills along the route built by Chinese coolies and Irish laborers, up into the rugged Sierra Nevada and over fabled Donner Pass. After a pause at the old railroad town of Truckee, Amtrak 6 glides eastward again, down slope along the beautiful Truckee River, across the Nevada state line, and into Reno. Finally, after a long day in the saddle, Jeff hands 6 off to his relief at Sparks, climbs down off the F59PHI and carries his grip to a waiting cab. After a mandatory rest, he'll get the two-hour call for a new assignment.

Operating Trains

This same story, with different characters, locomotives, and runs, is repeated thousands of times a day, all across North America. Engineers and conductors get their two-hour calls, collect their gear, and sign in at the yard. They climb up on F59 passenger locomotives, into GP15-1s, GP30s, SD45s, SD70MACs, M636s, big Dash 8s and 9s, and glittering AC4400CWs.

The railroading world looks a lot different from up in the right seat than at track side. So what do the engineers actually do up there? And what do they think about these big machines adored by the rail-fan community?

Stephen Priest

Stephen Priest and Mel Wilson both work for the Santa Fe, in the Kansas City West Seniority District, Eastern Division. They, like all the other engineers on the Santa Fe "call board," operate anything in the large varied locomotive fleet—everything from old GP7s and GP9s to the newest AC4400CWs. That gives them unique insights into the practical vices and virtues of individual makes and models out in the real world. Said Priest:

"Locomotives are each unique, as models and as individual units. You might get a SD40-2 one day that works fine, another SD40-2 later that is terrible—the result of how each has been used or abused. It always amazes me that locomotive consists work as well as they do, day to day. First, it is rare (except with yard switchers) that you have a single engine to work with—engines live their lives in consists, lashed together with other locomotives. These locomotives must 'talk' to each other, work together, function as a unified team. You can have GE and EMD units, new and old, all coupled together, and it doesn't always work perfectly. For one thing, you're always limited by the least-capable locomotive in the consist. If we have four brand-

The panel directly over Jeff Garrett's head controls the head-end-power generator, the power source for the lights, heat, and air-conditioning in the passenger cars astern. To the left of the head-end-power panel is the main computer display panel; the computer provides detailed information on the performance of the engine, electrical systems, and the whole locomotive.

new Dash 9s and one old Geep 7 in a consist, the Dash 9s will be somewhat limited to whatever the GP 7 can do—most of the Dash 9's potential will be wasted.

"A locomotive of any age is much more sophisticated than a car or truck. First, they are self-protective; if it gets too hot, for example, or loses oil pressure, the locomotive will automatically idle itself or shut itself down before major damage is done. And even if it is the fifth unit back from the lead, you know right away because the alarm bells start going off in the lead cab alerting you to a failure in your consist! The newest units will even tell you in detail what's happening on the computer screen. Thus, the locomotive monitors and protects itself, even without anybody in the cab.

"Although some railroads have attempted to maintain 'pure' lash-ups, it isn't usually practical to have just one make and model in a consist. Instead, railroads like Santa Fe design head-end power on a horsepower-per-ton basis. You want to run whatever you have available and to keep everything working all the time—that's what makes money. Some trains are assigned 1.2 horsepower per ton, for instance, while the really hot-shot trains get up to 12 horsepower per ton. This means that a consist will often have three big engines and one little one; that gets you over the road most efficiently.

"Locomotives are 'MUed' together [a slang expression based on 'multiple-unit' operation] with a 27-pin-connector MU cable and air line hoses, usually four. The electrical circuits control exterior lights, throttle position, reverser, and some emergency functions; the air lines control two different brake systems, the independent engine brakes and the train-line brakes

They call it the WhisperCab but if you try whispering in here at speed nobody will hear you. That's the computer display, bracketed by the audible alarm system on the left and the head-end-power panel on the right. You can cruise through the computer's displays by pressing the buttons below the screen—something that happens a lot when the computer elects to shut the locomotive down for some reason, real or imagined.

That guy way over on the other side of the cab is engineer Ed Gibson, piloting CalTrain 42 southbound out of San Francisco toward Silicon Valley. The F40s were part of the inspiration for the Canadian or wide cabs so common on new locomotives today. Those wide-open spaces are notoriously hard to heat, and the cab is pretty noisy, but you can slice right through a car running the gates and you'll stay on the tracks.

on all the cars. One of the hoses connects and equalizes all the air reservoirs on the locomotives. Another air line actuates the independent engine brakes. Some railroads have two sets of hoses on their power, one set left and one set right of the coupler; this is a preference and is not typical.

"Unlike rail fans, train crews have personal favorites based on what they're like to live on, work on, and run. For example, GE units sit higher and you have to climb more stairs to get to the cab. On the Santa Fe, the F45 and the FP45 'cowl'

units are really disliked by crews because they are very cold in winter and have a small heater. They are difficult to get into. The side doors require mountain climbing skills to enter the unit. Consequently, crews prefer to enter these cowl units through the nose door. This door makes it easier to lug your grip (meaning bag or satchel) into the behemoth. Older GP20s are great to work on because they have wide steps, low end platforms (good for grip wrestling), and excellent visibility. The SD40-2s are another crew favorite because of their huge end platforms. You could

Despite all the hype about the new wide cabs, the conventional design worn by Union Pacific 3619 is preferred by many train crews. Visibility is good, the controls are convenient, and you can put your feet up on the heater.

actually put up an umbrella and have a picnic for five on one of these vast decks.

"Until a few years ago, it was uncommon for the manufacturers to see much of their products once they left the factory. It was customary for railroads to maintain their own power, thus the builder did not see or categorize common defects in their products. Then, that changed with the 'power-by-the-hour' agreements and lease programs. Now, EMD and GE do the maintenance on their own products—and they get to see, immediately, the problems they could have overlooked in the past. Power-by-the-mile and power-by-the-hour contracts include requirements for high availability—95 percent or so—and the builders now have to meet that figure. The result has been a sudden burst of improvements to the latest designs, a factor in the current revolution in head-end-power technology that has made new locomotives a lot more reliable than in the past.

"The life of a locomotive engineer is really great, and Kansas City is a great place to work out of. On the Santa Fe, we have three basic runs: Kansas City to Newton, Kansas; from Kansas City to Wellington, Kansas; and from Kansas City to Arkansas City, Kansas. One is pretty flat, one is hilly, and one has a lot of curves—the variety keeps it interesting."

Getting Started

You fire up the big diesel engine of most modern locomotives back at the "equipment rack" inside the engine compartment. Move the start/stop switch to Engine Prime; this energizes the fuel pump, loads the injectors, and prepares the engine to start. Then rotate the control to the Start position, and huge storage batteries provide power to turn the engine against the tremendous compression. It seems to labor slowly for a few moments, then individual cylinders *chug* to life; the chugging gets faster as all the cylinders start to fire, warm up, and settle down to idle rpm.

The process of getting the train moving is fairly simple, but requires experience and judgment. On essentially level or slightly uphill terrain, the typical sequence for a train of moderate weight is as follows:

1. Automatic brake, if set, to Release.
2. Ensure that generator field is On.
3. Reverser to Forward.
4. Wait until the brakes on the rear cars have had a chance to begin releasing, approximately 15 seconds on a typical freight.
5. Throttle to Run 1, the first notch above Idle.
6. Gradually release independent engine brake with power applied to control speed (about .5 miles per hour) until all the coupler slack is taken up.
7. Monitor FRED (flashing rear-end device, also known as end-of-train device or ETD) for the signal indicating that the rear car is in motion.
8. Throttle to Run 2 until amperage begins to decline, then Run 3.
9. Monitor amperage to avoid more than 900 amps while starting. As amperage drops with train speed, increase throttle progressively (up to Run 8) or to maintain desired speed.

"You are essentially the manager of slack," engineer Mel Wilson said. "A typical 100-car freight train with standard draft gear will have 6 inches of slack for each car—50 feet of slack in the whole train. Before the trip we look at the train profile, which shows where the loaded and the empty cars are, the short cars

left
The GP60M is a wide-cab version of a four-axle locomotive, "Santa Fe's" first attempt to use the Canadian safety cab back in 1988. It added too much weight to the suspension of this particular model and crews objected to the resultant ride. It looks terrific, though, crossing the Missouri River at Sibley.

and the long cars, where the cushioned-underframe cars are in the manifest. You have to keep in mind the properties of each of these out on the road, going up and down hill or coming out of a 'sag.' You learn to modulate the throttle—backing off coming down off of a hill from Run 4 or 5 down to 3 or 2. This saves fuel, brake shoes, and wear and tear."

The engineer tests and evaluates the train as it builds speed, watching how it responds to throttle and brake, how heavy it feels, how the power in the consist responds. That will include testing the dynamic brake, if equipped. With a mile or more of cars stretched out astern, and all that slack, you've got to be careful about how you accelerate and brake—at the risk of breaking the train or "going on the ground." Sudden engine braking at the head-end can start a ripple through the train that, combined with the characteristics of light/heavy and long/short car combinations, can knock cars right off the rails. You want to know how the power on the point reacts long before you have a problem; that's why the engineer tests his train early in the trip.

Braking

With 50 or more feet of slack, all the different kinds of cars, and 7,000 tons of train snaking back behind you, it pays to be *very* careful about how and when you apply the brakes. There are three sets of brakes on the train: the dynamic brakes on the traction motors that only work when the train is in motion, the independent engine air brakes, and the train brake system that runs all the way back to the last car in

Dick Kruger is another Southern Pacific veteran of the steam age. He's conducting an air-brake test on a consist of three big AC4400s before sending them back out on the road. The layout of the AC4400 cab is somewhat different from the EMD version used on the SD70MAC and F59PHI.

the train, a mile or so behind you. So what do you do when that next signal is red?

"Well, first of all, you do not just get a red stop signal," said Wilson. "A flashing yellow will warn you to slow down, a clue that you're going to have to take a siding or hold the main to let another train past. The SOP [standard operating procedure] on the Santa Fe is to start with the dynamic brake to control the speed of the train, supplemented with the air. If you *have* to use the air, often all it takes is a minimum reduction from the automatic brake—6 to 8 pounds. Then you wait 20 or 30 seconds for the brakes to set up."

Because trains have tremendous momentum and very low rolling resistance, stopping a train takes time and distance. And controlling a heavy train on a downgrade is a challenge as old as railroading; if anything goes wrong with any

one of the three brake systems the result could be a wrecked train—it happens in the Rockies and Sierras with surprising frequency.

"When you're driving a train you either *create* or *inhibit* momentum," Wilson continued. "If I'm running along at 70 miles per hour and come up on a flashing yellow signal [indicating that the train should pass next signal at or below 40 miles per hour], I engage the dynamic brakes. If that doesn't seem to be slowing the train enough, I will keep the dynamics applied and then apply a 'first service' from the automatic air brake, taking mental note of the braking effect on the train. If at that time I feel the train is still not slowing quickly enough I will set more air [brakes] and this is accomplished by making a further or greater reduction from the automatic air brake. This in turn increases the braking effort of the entire train.

You normally take the siding at 35–40 miles per hour, slowing to a stop, hopefully with only the dynamics doing the braking. While the dynamics provide the most braking at about 10–25 miles per hour, they hardly help at all on speeds greater than 70 miles per hour. This is why engineers use air brakes to supplement the dynamic brakes. When slower speeds are reached, the automatic air brake is often released allowing the dynamic brakes to do most of the work.

An Uphill Battle

You can hear the battle between the crews and the mountains on your scanner in a dozen places in the western United States, and one of the best is at Palmer Lake, a lovely spot in the Colorado Rockies at about 7,000 feet where you can watch from track side while train crews scream at their locomotives.

When a heavy coal train, with new AC4400CWs on the point and a pair of helper locomotives pushing on the end, stalls, the crews share their misery on the radio. The engineer on the point calls back to the pushers to report that

A big GE leads the power on Conrail's TV-10 near Bear Mountain, New York. *Howard Ande*

next pages
Fifty years after the E-series locomotives started the process of retiring steam from American rails, a few creaky veterans are still soldiering along. Here's OCS-111 powering a Conrail director's special along the line near Bear Mountain, New York, on a bright, frigid day in January 1988. *Howard Ande*

That's a revitalized edition of ancient history on the rails in front of the Cannan, Connecticut, depot—an old RS3M, now belonging to the Housatonic Railroad. *Howard Ande*

the train is almost stalled on the grade, the turbocharger is overheating, and, with alarms going off, systems are shutting down. Turn on your scanner and listen to the trains:

"SP 220 to the helpers: Just to let you know, we're making about 10 miles per hour here, through Larkspur . . . and dwindling fast! The computer says, 'turbo intercooler water too hot,' over.

Now we've got main alarm bells, looks like we'll be stopping here north of the Larkspur crossing."

The delay on this occasion turns out to be fairly brief. The locomotive recovers its cool and SP 220 and its coal train soon are under way again. The process of getting a heavy coal train from mine to market is a battle the railroads have been fighting for over a hundred years.

And while the new locomotives are finally as powerful (as individual units) as the steam engines of old, it is still a battle to get over the Tehachapi, Cajon, Palmer Lake, Sherman Hill, and Horseshoe Curve grades.

Helpers or pushers provide assistance today, just as in the days of steam. Normally these little lash-ups are older locomotives—F45s, sometimes, or SD40-2s—stationed at the bottom of places like Cajon Pass or Horseshoe Curve. Even if the power on the point is sufficient to drag a heavy train up the hill, at some point the risk of coupler failure demands that somebody push from the back rather than pull from the front. And if there is any doubt about the issue, the helpers will stay hooked on for the downhill ride, too, providing dynamic braking to give the head-end power some margin of protection from a runaway.

End Of the Line

The trains push over the mountains, across the plains, from coast to coast and border to border—the hotshot freights, the "dog" locals, the trains carrying commuters, coal, cars, and all the other things that need to be moved from one place to another by rail. And although the trains keep going day and night, the crews work for 12 hours before they "die on the law." As the trips conclude, the trains drift into the yards at places like Green River, Wyoming, Wichita, Kansas, and hundreds of other places around the nation.

The two-hour call has come for new crews for the QNYLA, for the Coast Starlight, for the crews running the ancient GP7s in the Argentine Yard, for the slow freights and commuter runs up in Boston, along Long Island, and from New York to Washington, D.C.

The old GP7s and FL9s, the new AC4400s and SD70MACs, ease to a stop, and the tired crews climb down with their grips, and their empty Thermos bottles, and turn their trains over to the relief crews.

"Got a good set and release!" the radio says. "Highball from the Car Department! Have a good trip!"

The block signals turn from red to yellow or green; brakes to Off, reverse control goes to Forward. The throttle goes from Idle to Run 1, and the big engines sing a rising song as the ammeter needle dances up toward 1,000 amps; modulate the brake, modulate the throttle, monitor for wheel slip—the trains begin to move as the throttle moves up through the power settings: Run 2 . . . Run 3 . . . Run 8. Another trip begins for the people who run the trains.

Locomotive Schools and Suggested Reading

So . . . does it look like fun? Well, you too can learn to drive a locomotive (steam or diesel, big or small) at any one of several museums around the country.

The Feather River Rail Society at Portola, right by the Union Pacific main line in California's remote Feather River Canyon, will happily oblige with an hour of instruction on a ALCO S-1 or a sleek F7 "covered wagon" from the early days of dieselization. An hour on the S-1 is only $75 (at this writing) and an hour on both is only $175. And when the hot-shot Union Pacific freights zoom past you can wave to the guy in the Dash 9 from your perch at the control stand, one "hogger" to another.

Another great place for a check ride is the Nevada Northern's terrific program at East Ely, Nevada. Here you can operate a Baldwin steamer or one of the old Nevada Northern diesel switchers.

The Midland Railway of Baldwin, Kansas, can train you to be an engineer. You must be a member of the organization and are required to make student trips and pass various required tests as required by the Federal Railroad Administration. This process will typically take about a year.

Suggested Reading

The following periodicals all celebrate trains and locomotives, mostly the contemporary railroad industry. While not usually found on news racks (except at the biggest stands), they can often be found at hobby stores, particularly ones catering to model-train enthusiasts. We have a shop specializing in model trains in our community, and it stocks all but one of these publications; check your phone book for similar outlets.

Magazines

Extra 2200 South
PO Box 8110-820, Blaine, WA
98231-8110

Diesel Era
Withers Publishing
528 Dunkle School Road
Halifax, PA 17032

Trains
PO Box 1612
Waukesha, WI 53187

CTC Board— Railroads Illustrated
Hundman Publishing
13110 Beverly Park Road
Mukilteo, WA 98275

Pacific Rail News
PO Box 17108
North Hollywood, CA 91615

Flimsies
Shasta Rail Group
PO Box 7261
Chico, CA 95927-7261

Passenger Train Journal
PO Box 17108
North Hollywood, CA 91615

Railfan & Railroad
P.O. Box 700
Newark, NJ 07860

Railpace News Magazine
PO Box 927
Piscataway, NJ 08855-0927

Locomotive & Railway Preservation
PO Box 17108
North Hollywood, CA 91615

Railroad Press
1150 Carlisle Street, Suite 444
Hanover, PA 17331

Vintage Rails
PO Box 17108
North Hollywood, CA 91615

Consist: multiple locomotives connected together and controlled by the lead unit (see "lash-up").

Dog Train: slow, low-priority train that is likely to spend a lot of time "in the hole" waiting for "hot-shots."

Double Stack: a large car designed for carrying intermodal containers double-stacked; an essential component of the "land-bridge" transportation system that integrates ships, trucks, and trains.

Foamer: derisive railroad slang for extreme rail fans—people who seem to foam at the mouth at the sight of rare locomotives.

Hogback: a series of little up-and-down areas of terrain.

Hogger: a traditional term for engineers.

Hot-shot: a fast, high-priority freight train such as Santa Fe's 199 from Chicago to Richmond, California.

In the Hole: railroad slang for waiting on a siding for another train to pass.

Lash-Up: multiple locomotives connected by electrical and pneumatic lines, controlled by one engineer.

MU: multiple-unit interconnection system for locomotives, an electrical-pneumatic system that allows up to ten, or even more, locomotives to function as one huge unit.

Oil Can: railroad slang for the tank car.

Point: lead or front locomotive; the "power on the point" is the first locomotive in a consist.

Power: engineer slang for a locomotive or a consist.

Power Assembly: an individual engine cylinder assembly, easily removable.

Prime Mover: occasional manufacturing and common rail-fan term for the diesel engine.

Reefer: railroad slang for the refrigerator car.

Run or Notch: the throttle setting, from 1 (first notch above idle, about 100 rpm on EMDs or 150 rpm on GEs) to 8 (full power, about 950 rpm on EMDs or 1,050 on GEs).

Sag: the bottom of a grade followed by an uphill section of track.

Sub: subdivision—an area of local responsibility, traditionally about 150 miles of track.

To Die on the Law: to exceed the maximum 12 hours of service before reaching your destination; then you stop the train, call the dispatcher, and wait for a taxi to show up with a relief crew.

Index